Doris Hardie

Timothy Hamm

Rosemary Daniell

Julie Suk

Jessie Schell

John Carr

Guy Owen

Barbara Lovell

William Harmon

WHITE TRASH

WHITE

THE NEW SOUTH COMPANY
1226 Dilworth Road
Charlotte, North Carolina 28203

TRASH

*An Anthology
of Contemporary Southern Poets*

EDITED BY NANCY STONE AND ROBERT WATERS GREY

For Alexander, Catherine, and Kent

ACKNOWLEDGMENTS

JAMES APPLEWHITE "Discardings" (appeared in American Poetry Review); "Combat Station" (appeared in Virginia Quarterly Review); and "Drinking Music" (appeared in Poetry Now) are reprinted by permission of the Author. "Driving Through a Country That is Vanishing" (first appeared under the title "Driving through the Country America that is Vanishing") is reprinted by permission of Esquire Magazine © 1972 by Esquire, Inc.

COLEMAN BARKS "New Words" appeared in Carolina Quarterly and is reprinted by permission of the Editor. "Big Toe," "Upper Lip," and "Liver" from The Juice copyright © 1972 by Coleman Barks are reprinted by permission of Harper & Row, Publishers, Inc. "Navel" and "Brain" by Coleman Barks, first appeared in Quickly Aging Here, Some Poets of the 1970s, a Doubleday-Anchor Book, edited by Geof Hewitt.

DAVID BOTTOMS "All Systems Tower and Collapse" appeared in Southern Poetry Review and is reprinted by permission of the Editor.

FRED CHAPPELL "February" from The World Between The Eyes, Louisiana State University Press, 1971, and "Cleaning the Well" from River, Louisiana State University Press, 1975, are reprinted by permission of the Author and the Publisher.

KELLY CHERRY "Phylogenesis" (appeared in The Anglican Theological Review) and "Natural Theology" (appeared in Abba, A Journal of Prayer) are reprinted by permission of the Author.

ROSEMARY DANIELL "The Operation" and "A Week in February" are from A Sexual Tour of the Deep South, Copyright © 1964, 1969, 1972, 1973, 1974, 1975 by Rosemary Daniell. Reprinted by permission of Holt, Rinehart and Winston, Publishers.

ROBERT WATERS GREY "Burning" (appeared in Miscellany) and "Search for Victims" (from Writing About Literature and Film, Bryan and Davis, Harcourt Brace Jovanovich, Inc., 1975) are reprinted by permission of the Author. "Stern Shapes" appeared in Southern Poetry Review and is reprinted by permission of the Editor. "The First" appeared in The Cold Mountain Review and is reprinted by permission of the Editor.

WILLIAM HARMON Sections from Treasury Holiday copyright © 1969, 1970 by William Harmon are reprinted by permission of Wesleyan University Press.

RODNEY JONES "Extensions of Watts Bar Dam" (appeared in a somewhat different form as "Watts Bar Dam") copyright by Shenandoah is reprinted from Shenandoah, The Washington and Lee University Review by permission of the Editor.

BARBARA LOVELL "The Pireaus Apollo" appeared in The Cold Mountain Review and is reprinted by permission of the Editor. "The Fern" appeared in Crucible and is reprinted by permission of the Editor.

ADRIANNE MARCUS "She Calls From Shore" (originally appeared in Motive); "A Formality of Love" (originally appeared in Poetry Northwest); and "The Woman In The Next Room" (originally appeared in Pacific Sun) are from The Moon Is A Marrying Eye, Red Clay Books, and are reprinted by permission of the Author.

HEATHER McHUGH "Spring" and "Leaving" (appeared in Antioch Review) are reprinted by permission of the Author.

HEATHER MILLER "Lumbee Children" (originally appeared in *Pembroke Magazine*) and "The Vinegar Jug" are from *Horse Horse Tyger Tyger, Red Clay Books*, and are reprinted by permission of the Author.

MICHAEL MOTT "Path Under the Medlars" appeared in *Southern Poetry Review* and is reprinted by permission of the Editor.

PAUL NEWMAN The *Paula* section (originally appeared under the title "Gomera" copyright 1974 by *Shenandoah* is reprinted from *Shenandoah, The Washington and Lee University Review* by permission of the Editor) is from *Paula*, Dragon's Teeth Press, 1975. "Washington Diseased" appeared in *The New River Review* and is reprinted by permission of the Editor.

GUY OWEN "The Old Men," "Afterwards," and "The White Stallion" are from *The White Stallion and Other Poems*, John F. Blair, Publisher, 1969, and are reprinted by permission of the Author.

JESSIE SCHELL "Burning the Letters" and "To the Children Selling Lightning Bugs" (appeared in *The Greensboro Review*); "The Blessing" (appeared in *Southern Poetry Review*); and "Delta Summer" (appeared in *The Dragonfly*) are reprinted by permission of the Author.

JAMES SEAY "The Majorette on the Self-Rising Flour Sign," "Water I Thought Sweet and Deep," "No Man's Good Bull," and "Grabbling in Yokna Bottom" copyright © 1968, 1970 by James Seay. Reprinted from *Let Not Your Hart*, by permission of Wesleyan University Press.

R. T. SMITH "Waking Under Sun" (originally appeared in *Southern Poetry Review*) is from *Waking Under Snow*, The Cold Mountain Press, and is reprinted by permission of the Author.

JOHN STONE "Looking Down Into a Ditch" (appeared in *Inlet*); "Losing a Voice in Summer" (appeared in *Poetry Northwest*); and "Double-Header" (appeared in *The American Scholar*) are reprinted by permission of the Author.

NANCY STONE "Quest" appeared in *The Greensboro Review* and is reprinted by permission of the Author.

DABNEY STUART "Arrival," "Major Work," "The Trial," and "New Year's" are from *The Other Hand*, Louisiana State University Press, 1974, and are reprinted by permission of the Author and the Publisher.

JULIE SUK "Rabid" appeared in *The St. Andrews Review* and is reprinted by permission of the Author.

ROSS TALARICO "Frayed Sheets" (appeared in *Granite*) and "Surgeon's Prayer" (appeared in *New Letters*) are reprinted by permission of the Author.

MARVIN WEAVER "Crazy Horse" (appeared in *The St. Andrews Review*) and "The Hunt" (appeared in *The Hollins Critic*) from *Hearts and Gizzards*, Curveship Press are reprinted by permission of the Author.

JONATHAN WILLIAMS "Dealer's Choice and the Dealer Shuffles" from *An Ear in Bartram's Tree*, University of North Carolina Press, 1969; "The Autochthon," "Dear Reverend Carl C. McIntire," from *The Loco Logodaedalist in Situ*, Cape Goliard/Grossman, 1972, are reprinted by permission of the Author. "Who Is Little Enis?" from *Elite/Elate Poems*, Grossman Publishers, 1976, is reprinted by permission of the Author.

CHARLES WRIGHT "Equation" (appeared in *Pomegranate Press Broadside*); "January" and "Indian Summer" (appeared in *Chicago Review*); "Next" (appeared in *Occident*); "At Zero" (appeared in *The Ohio Review*); and "Morandi" (appeared in *Field*) are reprinted by permission of the Author. "Sentences" is reprinted by permission; © 1976 The New Yorker Magazine, Inc.

Photographs Kelly Cherry by Michael C. Wootton, Rosemary Daniell by Jonathan Coppelman, Robert Waters Grey by Gayle Petrakis, Adrianne Marcus by Warren Marcus, Nancy Stone by Kent Fuqua, Marvin Weaver by Steve Aldridge, Jonathan Williams by Charles R. McNeill, Charles Wright by Holly Wright, Doris Hardie by Ken Millette, John Carr by Marjorie Bendl, Michael Mott by Gene Ellis.

Cover by John Thornton.

Don't Try and Sell Me No Pink Flamingos:
AN INTRODUCTION

Naturally I would a whole lot rather be back there among the pages of this book, paid up and in good standing, instead of up here in the front talking about it.

That, my friends, is the truth, but it is also (even though phonetics are not indicated by spelling) a genuine trashy sentence. Not *tacky*, mind you. There is a big difference. Some southern writers would rather die slowly and badly than admit to a touch of trash. They will go to great lengths to deny there's any such (of a) thing as a Cracker in their gene pool or a Redneck in the woodpile. But the truth is every southerner has a streak of trash just as every selfsame southerner has a drop (just a tad) of Plantagenet blood. Some have the strength of character and well-developed mixed feelings (what the editors fairly enough call "irony") to admit it and even enjoy it. Those who don't are just tacky, no matter how elegant and refined and aesthetic they may seem to outsiders—Yankees and such. There are some celebrated southern public stances which are, really, the literary equivalent of planting pink flamingos in the front yard. Point is, all southerners equally have deep roots and plenty of ancestors. Mostly we are kin to each other. And we have always had mixed feelings about that and the South. People, including a lot of tacky southerners, keep telling us that the southern literary "renaissance" is all over and done with, long gone. Read the poets here, good poets and true (and, praise be, more various in voice than any anthology I've seen for a good while), and you'll agree that the negative critics, the doubters and scoffers, are as wrong as wrong can be. I am familiar with the work of some of these poets. Some are old friends and friends of friends, and several are, I'm pleased to say, former students. Others, like the talented student writers, Timothy Hamm and Doris Hardie, are new to me. These are all worthy folks. Of course there's a gracious plenty of other eligible southern poets, of all ages and stages, who are not here and are every bit as good as anybody who is. That is always the way it is and has to be. But in this case you can honestly say they are well served and represented by what is here. (That is not always or even often the case with anthologies.) What's here is good enough for anybody. I feel like having some bumper stickers printed up—HONK IF YOU LOVE FRED CHAPPELL, BLINK YOUR LIGHTS IF YOU BELIEVE IN COLEMAN BARKS;

CAUTION I BRAKE FOR ARMADILLOS AND JOHN CARR. And so on. Or maybe to stand up at some session of Literary Holy Rollers and holler: "Everybody who loves poetry say after me—James Seay and Kelly Cherry and Rosemary Daniell!" All the poets, and the editors, are to be thanked and congratulated.

As a Southerner my (own) self, now living in Maine, I'm very happy to have this book to pass around to my friends up here. The climate is a lot different and so is the accent, but the people who live here are a lot like us. Also for other kinds of Americans, from the high-priced spread of the Northeast, from the Middlewest and West, all those who may be trying to solve the mystery of our next President from Plains, Georgia, these poems will tell you all as much as you need and deserve to know. I imagine Jimmy would be in the book, too, if he knew how to write poems. Matter of fact, just in case (it's been known to happen) he moves into the White House and starts to get the Big-head and forget his real roots, he'd be well advised to keep a copy of this book handy. And so would you and I.

George Garrett
York Harbor, Maine
July 1976

FOREWORD

Turnip greens, turnip greens,
  Good old turnip greens,
Cornbread and buttermilk,
  And good old turnip greens.

We spent an afternoon earlier this year in a room full of writers, editors, and publishers who were gathered to discuss Southern writing. At the beginning there was the assumption that a thing called Southern writing exists. Two hours later a writer-feminist from northern Sweden was standing on her chair shouting at a writer-male chauvinist from Denver. Every definition of Southern writing offered had been shouted down. No one had mentioned continuity or irony. No one had mentioned language.

The Southerners present fell out of the discussion early. One of the panelists, a descendant of a Confederate general, spoke two sentences and wisely shut up when another panelist furiously accused Southerners of not facing their history. "Shows you how thin the culture is," sniffed one New York writer. "No Southerner today can write in the South," said another.

That debacle showed, among other things, that Southern writing is more difficult to define and that it is even more vigorous than it was twenty years ago. It became prominent and recognizable because it focused on and explored the American experience with motifs of place, time, and character that recurred until they became one with the themes they carried. Isolation, the disintegration of the family dynasty, the ascendency of graceless materialism over genteel poverty signalled: this is about the South. Thanks to the proliferation of small presses independent of universities, topics assumed to be Southern have surfaced in minority and regional writing in all parts of the country, and everyone now knows that idiocy, alcoholism, homosexuality, incest, miscegenation, and castrating females exist elsewhere.

Two other happenings are probable sources of inspiration for *White Trash*. One, the plethora of minority anthologies—both stories and poems—that have come across our desks in recent years made us want to bring out a much-neglected group. We suspect, though, that white trash is not a minority, except in the sense of being overworked, underpaid, unorganized, its wishes largely ignored by the eastern intellectual establishment. Two, if the news media, the philosophers of the instantaneous, continue to tout the Sun Belt, the South can expect a tsunami of tourists, retirees, and industry. White trash may then be in for the kind of attention that invites sayings from a lot of fake trash, so that anybody who can imitate William Faulkner or Tennessee Williams will be put into a book. We see it already.

There is still, however, in the sameness of contemporary America with its affluence, education, its mass communication and distribution, an authentic kind of writing that can be said to belong to the Southern region and no other. Although some of the poets who answered our call weren't born below the Mason-Dixon Line, each of these has been nurtured at some time by the South; the language, the history, the spirit, and the humor are integrated in their work. All exhibit the wit and irony necessary to meld tradition and change; their individuality is apparent, yet they have not repudiated their past. All are living. We predict that many have their best work ahead of them. Their inexhaustible energy indicates a continuation of the old "root hog or die" spirit. Present are the language traditions, nurtured and preserved in the history and folk wisdom of a people who have lived continuously, although not always harmoniously, for 350 years on the same land. These traditions occur in vigorous, contemporary forms, in an unaffected voice authentic by virtue of its direct connection to the old songs, games, and riddles of the region which lead into ways of understanding that are unique.

Some of the poems are previously unpublished. Naturally, we have chosen from our published favorites. Limitations of space and money forced us to leave out many poems that we like and many poets, too. We could have had more poems from fewer poets, but a broad scope is one of our aims at this time. We are pleased to be the first to present this book of poetry springing from tensions readily observable in the South today between tradition and change, between colloquial and literary forms. We believe that these poems will survive and that the poets included will continue to have an important effect on the nature of poetry which transcends regional boundaries.

Nancy Stone and Robert Waters Grey
Dilworth Community
Charlotte, North Carolina
Summer, 1976

CONTENTS

WHITE TRASH

Discardings

Sometimes going back toward together I find
Me with lost, no-count, low-down and lonely:
Single with trees in logged-over evening,
Sun on us bound to go down.

Things lying low are sipped by the weather.
Black-strap creeks seem a slow molasses
Toward horizons thirsty with gravity.

Today in trees I kicked an old bucket
Full of woes, the chipped enamel like knotholes.
Burrows raised lids under leaves; quick fur
Eyes were on my face. Under the trash pile
I heard them like trickles of water,
Tunneling the sun down.

Home, when I pour bourbon and remember
A holed rubber boot on a hill of leaves,
It must be their sounds I am drinking.

I salute a boot from the foot
Of an unheralded cavalry. A black man
Walked furrows behind a mule whole years, unhorsed
By no war but the sun against the moon.

I drink branch water and bourbon
To the boards of his house that the wind
Has turned to its color and taken entirely.

Driving Through a Country That Is Vanishing

It begins to snow in a country
Between the past and what I see,
Soft flakes like eyelids softly descending,
Closing about branches, orchards of pecans,
Like washpot soot streaked in lines on the sky

Or is it that these husks empty of nuts
Are moving upward among the flakes they have suspended,
Like eyesockets gaping or a mockery of birds

So that a girl by the name of Mary Alice Taylor
Sings across this air from the seventh grade.
"Billie he come to see me. Billie he come
Last night." A mole, color of clear skin,
Swims by her nose. Flakes condense the light.

"Billie he asked me to be his wife, 'course I said alright."

Snow as if holding the country houses
Apart to be inspected, unsilvered
Mirror that lets float out of its depths
As from an old ocean of no dimension
Unlimited objects, leather tack and
Spokes of surreys, china
Long broken, whittled horses
Everything their hands would have touched.

Combat Station

Ralph with the corded triceps, with cleft chest wired
With black hair, told Marine Corps war. I wielded the spanner.
Our lift in the open sun made all metal stinging
In heat-thin oil. His talk was Australian women,
Severed American heads on a path in New Guinea.
The lens of an August atmosphere focused our labor.
Beads of tractors' rims were loosened with wedges.
We greased trailers and pick-ups, washed clay rivers
From rusted fenders in the waning afternoons.
At his headquarters desk where a cash register rang,
My father gave orders to receive the new assaults of customers.
We fought against being overrun, held wave after wave,
Fired slugs into chassis from the automatic greasegun,
My brother riddling fenders with a high-pressure hose.
No matter how we mauled at wedges, levered with tire tools,
Tugged at exhaust pipes blazing like machine guns,
Our general denied us victory by selling to the enemy.
Like heroes we fought for a stalemate, held out for sundown.
Staring into hubcaps, I remembered the metal of a P-47
That had cut through a grove of pines and broken in a field,
Pilots' blood jellied in the cockpit. My father's silhouette
Tightened the close-ringed horizon of trees, as I fought on
For the moment we could signal a roof above the gas pumps
To blaze up its pantheon of bulbs into creek-water evening,
When field moths would orbit their wattage like foliage in motion.

Drinking Music

I

Cornstalks and arrowheads, wood rot cleanly as wash
In wind. They are covered by this roof as I think:
The loosers, the fallen, the kind who go under, faces
As at home in an imagination of soil as Civil War casualties;
Whiskey workers I've known with remnant teeth,
Men from down home, 'ol country boys whose lace boots
Are well made and everything else shows khaki or denim
Scrubbed by rain in summer and underbrush fall
So the sand white cotton shines through.

These men are for the showing of true colors,
They live where sun-slant instills into fields
And its red clay hue crests up into a waving of broom sedge,
Sweet potatoes below clot into a succulence like blood.

Their ears are given over for all time (each night)
To a slow-poured juke of excuse: the molasses consolation
of Hank Williams' songs. The twanged words seem physical
As pork chops and greens from turnips. The only whiskey
Forgiveness there is. Paul Junior Taylor with your Budweiser
Belly, your tackle's shoulders, where are you now?

II

The broom sedge fields were ruddy from sunset.
Cold whiskey is the color of straw.
Sky ain't hardly kept no color at all,
And Lord I'm lonely for the ground.
I'm far from home but near.
I'm high, so high and low. Sweet chariot.

The song is rich and red, like what men eat.
Sky is clear as the ninety proof shine they drink.
Lord, Lord, a man is a funny piece of meat.
Their boots are good in fields that understand their feet.

from **New Words**

3.
The face does look like an ear, eventually.
Words we're using now
burn out. What the point is
I don't know. There's not a word in English
for that time when the world
will not exist. The Maoris have one,
both for when there wasn't life
and when there won't be:
Po.

p-o in the OED
means peacock and small devil,
origin unknown.

pollex—the innermost digit of the forelimb
in air-breathing vertebrates, the thumb.
Whales have thumbs.

polroz—the pit under a waterwheel.

pome as a verb, to form a compact head or heart,
as a cabbage that pomes close to the ground.

potamic—of rivers,
and things that live there, like turtles,
moons, waterwheels, cabbages,
and words that hold an image
for a moment
before they turn to sand
and silver paint.

4.
Backwards from the center
with the M volume.

musophobist—one who regards poetry
with suspicious dislike.

muskin—pretty face, sweetheart.

mimp—to purse up one's mouth, primly
in silence. She just sits there
with her muskin all mimped up.

melrose—a curative preparation
made of powdered rose leaves, honey, and alcohol.
When she looks like that,
give her some melrose.

meaze—the form that a rabbit leaves
pressed in the grass
and comes home to.

maris—the womb.

mally—dotingly fond. Mally father
maketh wicked child.

mahu—a name for the devil.

macilent—thin and shriveled from poverty

Taking such small steps down the list,
alphabetically disguising
the way I say the same thing over and over:

How this is where I hide.

In a room with thirteen dictionaries
and no windows,
hide from women
who love more than I can stand
to be loved,
who want me not to hide
inside the breath of an old word,
or inside their bodies
like St. Elmo's fire
playing under the shoulder blades.

Rabelais, St. Francois,
help me out.

fanfreluche—to trifle, to act wantonly. Fanfreluching it,
thirty times a day.

grimp—to climb energetically, using hands and feet.
How the little grimper made it, I'll never know.

griggles—small apples left on the tree
by the gatherer, for the children to have.

granons—the whiskers of a cat.
Cut the granons off one side,
she'll walk in a circle.

glore—loose fat. Strange to see
two eyes waking up
in the midst of all that glore.

gillian—a flirty, feisty girl.
and right under,

gillian-a-burnt-tail, will-o-the-wisp,
a little phosphorescence in the swamp.

5.
barnaby—the 11th of June, St. Barnabus' day, the longest
under the old calendar, hence anything long and drawn out.

battologist—someone who repeats himself a lot. From Battos,
the stammering man
who went to ask the Delphic oracle
about his voice, and all she said was,
You shall become a king in Libya.
He kept asking *What about my voice,*
Wh-What about my voice.

Now his name is the front half
to a word nobody uses.

And he one of the chief personalities
in a listpoem, of what
we no longer have in common.

6.
ferdful—either awesome, inspiring fear,
or full of fear, or both. *Is anybody down there,*
he shouted ferdfully. *Yes,* came back
the ferdful answer.

feriation—a cessation of work, the act of keeping
a holiday. Simple feriation was enough for the weekend.
No binges, no feasts.

fernshaw—a thicket of ferns.
Secret places along creeks
around Chattanooga
were fernshaws, and nobody knew it.

fid—a small but thick piece of anything,
as a fid of cheese, or hamburger.

fidibus—a paper match for lighting pipes.

from **Body Poems**

Big Toe

running running
running but clean
as a referee's whistle

& absolutely still
within my shoe
inside my sock:

he listens for mud

Navel

hold the phone
down here see
if she can still
hear me gurgling:

my Long Distance
mother

Brain

a flashlight
looking through the empty
limbs

Upper Lip

the pronouns
keep changing
from *myself*
to *yourself*
and back:

during a long kiss

Liver

a dripping locker room
full of older men

The Finger of Necessity

Postal Area #29 Los Angeles

Twice recently young girls have
        given me the finger. The
    first was on the freeway, she

sitting close to her boyfriend turned
        with sure purpose and aimed
    at prominence, seat-belted in

two lanes over. The chemical shock to
        my system made me feel so
    like they wanted I chased them

for miles trying to think of something
        to yell back. The second a few
    minutes ago standing beside a

drugstore would have been easy to
        go back by but I just waved
    like oh another one. It must

be something in the atmosphere, Scorpio
        on the ascendant, or maybe they
    were bored with the just looking

and better this than what I didn't give,
        much better. With one buzzoff
    finger she became the mother

of my invention with her red
        shirt and her hip-huggers
    and her flowered viny belt:

Hey cat lady, you eat it.

All Systems Tower and Collapse

for Tom Trimble

This should be a night for beer and good talk
or Tennessee whiskey and motel whores,
but tonight I drink and lie here alone
listening to walls say others have found
better company to share their darkness.
From the nightstand by the bed Gideons
offer me the company of old words,
but their premise is all wrong. So is yours
and any philosophy that demands
the found absolute of any method.
Here's the natural gospel of it all:
all systems tower and collapse, and we
babble in darkness seeking foundations
for other reconstructions, knowing all
along that what works always is nothing.

Jamming with the Band at the VFW

I played old Country and Western
then sat alone at a table near the bandstand,
smug in the purple light that seemed like a bruised sun
going down over Roswell, Georgia.

A short bald man in a black string tie
and a woman with a red beehive
waltzed across the floor
like something out of Lawrence Welk,
his hips moving like a metronome in baggy pants,
hers following like a mirror image.

For a long time I watched and drank beer,
listened to the tear-jerking music,
thought of all my written words,
all the English classes, the workshops,
the MA stored safely under my cowboy hat,
the arty sophisticates and educated queers
who attend poetry readings in Atlanta

and weighed against them
not one bald man waltzing a woman through another Blitz,
but all men turning gray who dream of having died
at Anzio, Midway, Guadalcanal.

Then rising from my chair
I drank the last of the Pabst
and moved through the bruised light of the bandstand
onto the purple dance floor, toward the tables
across the room, toward the table beside the bar,
and there the woman with platinum hair
and rhinestone earrings, moving suddenly toward me.

Proofreading at the Picayune: *I*

We proofreaders have eyes like Choctaw bonepickers:
Catch extra letters, all caps, no caps
And wrong caps, censorious fingers crosshatching,
Squiggling, slashing, sending surplus characters
Looping in tailspins off the margin to limbo.
We penetrate New Pork's disguise,
Are amazed at advice to "keep eyes
And arse open," run Aries columns
In Gemini boxes (find your lover strange lately?)
And in general ride herd on the reported world.
And when too big with pride, remember
The moon landing and the day a packed bus
Ran into the river below Waterproof, La.
ASTRONUTS LAND ON MOON
16 WATERPROOF NEGROES DROWN

Sic transit armadillo

Even the armadilloes know: the New
Ice Age is coming—but it won't catch
Them. They left this Delta eden before
The Great War trekking north to the corn
Deserts of the Midwest but now—one horny
Foot in front of the other—are shuffling
Back to the garden. Behind the teasing birds
Racing the seasons, but coming anyway,
Informed by the mean number of freezing days
Registered on the racial memory
That paradise can be revisited. Maybe the future
Can be escaped, even by the slow.

A scout lies dead in this tulip patch
Between town and the levee, neatly
Decapitated by the old woman stranger
To the tribe who bid her grandmother goodbye,
Its head in the grass, the journey frozen on its eyes:
Paddling over from Arkansas, breasting
The great river remembering Iowa, mud, willows,
Sniffing the warm innocent past
As it topped the levee, loping happily
Into the land of the tree of dark and light.
But the sentry'd forgotten password and parole.

Eden may not be revisited with impunity.
Your name has not been recorded, only given.
The recusants are leprous at Carville
The settled generation is freezing in the cornfields
The ones who try to return will be served up fried.
Truly, we all have the same problems:
The past is a lying whore and the present fickle
And the future has crossed us off her list.
But anyway there's a lesson here for the polar bears.
Somewhere.

February

Wouldn't drive and wouldn't be led,
So they tied cotton line around its neck and it backed,
Clipped steps, as the rope stretched.
Whereat,
They shot it clean through the shrieking brain.
And it dropped in a lump.

                            The boy, dismayed
With delight, watches the hog-killing,
Sharply alive in its tangle. Recoils,
Tries to hold it sensible; fails;
All the meaning in a brutal hour.

They bring the sledge down, and difficult
With the horse plunging white-eyed, hoofs
Askitter in the slick steep bank; the blood-smell's
Frightful and he snorts, head clatters back.
The pig's still gently quivering,
                   he's got a blue and human eye.
Lug it over and tumble it on, and the horse
Goes straining. The men swear
And grin, their teeth show hard in piercing air.

               Frost gauzy on leaf and stone,
               The sky but faintly blue, wiped white.

. . . And into the yard. The fire popping and licking,
They roll the big black cauldron to it. Saturday,
The neighbor women and men and kids, the faces
Broad with excitement. Wow wow across the gravel,
The cast iron pot; settles on the flame,
Black egg in its scarlet nest. Dark speech of the men,
Women waiting silent, hands under the blue aprons.

Long spike rammed through the heels
And up he goes against the big-armed oak
And dipped down in, dipped again, so

His hair falls off. (Swims in the filmed water
Like giant eyelashes.) Like a silver gourd
His belly shines and bulges. He's opened
And his steam goes up white,
The ghost of hog in the glassy morning.
They catch his guts.

                          The child, elated-drunk
With the horror, as they undo joint
And joint, stands with the men, watches
Their arms. They yank and slash, stammer
Of blood on the denim, eyelets of blood
On arm and fabric. They laugh like scythes,
Setting the head aside to see the dismantling
With its own blue eyes—still smiles
A thin smug smile!

                         And they cleave it
And cleave it. Loins. Ham.
                      Shoulder. Feet. Chops.
Even the tail's an obscure prize.
Goes into buckets; the child hauls
From hand to hand the pail all dripping.
Top of the heap, tremulous as water, lies
The big maroon liver.

                      And the women receive it.
Gravely waiting as for supper grace.

The kitchen is glossy with heat, surcharged
With the smell of hog. Every surface
Is raddled with the fat. He slides
His fingers on the jamb, it feels like flesh.
The whole lower house juicy with hog,
A bit of it in every cranny.
Where does it all come from?
                      (A most unlikely prodigious pig.)
And now the women, busy, talk
Within the great clouds of oil and steam, bared

Elbows, heads nodding like breezy jonquils.
Clash of kettles, spoons
Yammering in the bowls, the windows opaque gray
With pig.

The sun reaches under the tree. They're gleaning
The last of him and the slippery whiskey jar
Goes handily among them. Wipe their mouths
With greasy wrists. And the smug head
Burst and its offerings distributed. Brain.
Ears. And the tail handed off with a clap of laughter.
They lick the white whiskey and laugh.

And his bladder and his stomach sack! puffed
Up and tied off and flung to the kids,
Game balls, they bat them about,
Running full tilt head down across the scattered yard.
And then on a startled breeze
The bladder's hoist, vaults high and gleams in the sunlight
And reflects on its shiny globe
The sky a white square
And the figures beneath, earnest figures
Gazing straight up

Cleaning the Well

Two worlds there are. One you think
You know; the Other is the Well.
In hard December down I went.
"Now clean it out good." Lord, I sank
Like an anchor. My grand-dad leant
Above. His face blazed bright as steel.

Two worlds, I tell you. Swallowed by stones
Adrip with sweat, I spun on the ache
Of the rope; the pulley shrieked like bones
Scraped merciless on violins.
Plunging an eye. Plunging a lake
Of corkscrew vertigo and silence.

I halfway knew the rope would break.

Two suns I entered. At exact noon
The white sun narrowly hung above;
Below, like an acid floating moon,
The sun of water shone.
And what beneath that? A monster trove

Of blinding treasure I imagined:
Ribcage of drowned warlock gleaming,
Rust-chewed chain mail, or a plangent
Sunken bell tolling to the heart
Of earth. (They'd surely·chosen an art-
less child to sound this soundless dreaming

O.) Dropping like a meteor,
I cried aloud—"Whoo! It's *God
Damn* cold!"—dancing the skin of the star.
"You watch your mouth, young man," he said.
I jerked and cursed in a silver fire
Of cold. My left leg thrummed like a wire.

Then, numb. Well water rose to my waist
And I became a figure of glass,
A naked explorer of outer space.
Felt I'd fricasseed my ass.
Felt I could stalk through earth and stone,
Nerveless creature without a bone.

Water-sun shattered, jelly-
bright wavelets lapped the walls.
Whatever was here to find, I stood
In the lonesome icy belly
Of the darkest vowel, lacking breath and balls,
Brain gummed mud.

"Say, Fred, how's it going down there?"
His words like gunshots roared; re-roared.
I answered, "Well—" (*Well well well* . . .)
And gave it up. It goes like Hell,
I thought. Precise accord
Of pain, disgust, and fear.

"Clean it out good." He drifted pan
And dipper down. I knelt and dredged
The well floor. Ice-razors edged
My eyes, the blackness flamed like fever,
Tin became nerve in my hand
Bodiless. *I shall arise never.*

What did I find under this black sun?
Twelve plastic pearls, monopoly
Money, a greenish rotten cat,
Rubber knife, toy gun,
Clock guts, wish book, door key,
An indescribable female hat.

Was it worth the trip, was it true Descent?
Plumbing my childhood, to fall
Through the hole in the world and become . . .
What? *He told me to go. I went.*
(Recalling something beyond recall.
Cold cock on the nether roof of Home.)

Slouch sun swayed like a drunk
As up he hauled me, up, up,
Most willing fish that was ever caught.
I quivered galvanic in the taut
Loop, wobbled on the solid lip
Of earth, scarcely believing my luck.

His ordinary world too rich
For me, too sudden. Frozen blue,
Dead to armpit, I could not keep
My feet. I shut my eyes to fetch
Back holy dark. Now I knew
All my life uneasy sleep.

Jonah, Joseph, Lazarus,
Were you delivered so? Ript untimely
From black wellspring of death, unseemly
Haste of flesh dragged forth?
Artemis of waters, succor us,
Oversurfeit with our earth.

My vision of light trembled like steam.
I could not think. My senses drowned
In Arctic Ocean, the Pleiades
Streaked in my head like silver fleas.
I could not say what I had found.
I cannot say my dream.

When life began re-tickling my skin
My bones shuddered me. Sun now stood
At one o'clock. Yellow. Thin.
I had not found death good.
"Down there I kept thinking I was dead."

"Aw, you're all right," he said.

Phylogenesis

She cracks her skin
like a shell, and goes in

She camps in her womb
She sucks the marrow from her bones

and sips bison's blood
in the afternoon; for years,

snow piles outside the cave she burrows in
She wakes to warm weather,

fur on her four feet, grass
rising and falling in waves like water

She feeds on flowering plants,
enjoys a cud of orchid and carrot

In the Middle Permian, scales slippery as shale appear
on her back; her spine unfurls a sail broadside

to the sun, filling with a light like wind, while *Sphenodon*
turns its third eye on the sky, sensing

rain, and rock salt washes into the ocean
Silent as mist, she slides down a mud bank on her underbelly

She's lobe-finned and fleshy,
pumping air through her gills

She's soft as jelly
Her skull is limestone

She drifts, like a continent
or protozoan, on the planet's surface,

and sinks into the past
like a pebble into a brackish pool

The seas catch fire
The earth splits and gapes

The earth cracks open like an egg
and she goes in

We begin

Natural Theology

You read it in the blue wind,
the blue water, the rock spill,
the blue hill

rising like a phoenix from ash. Some mind
makes itself known through the markings of light
on air; where earth rolls, right

comes after, our planet's bright spoor. . . . If you look,
        you'll find
truth etched on the tree trunk,
the shark's tooth, a shell, a hunk

of root and soil. Study from beginning to end.
Alpha and omega—these are the cirrus alphabet,
the Gnostics' cloudy "so—and yet."

If a tree falls in a forest, a scared hind
leaps, hearing branches break;
you crawl under the log and shake

honey out of a hollow, eggs from a nest, ants from the end
of a stick; resting, you read God's name on the back of a bass
in a blue pool; God grows everywhere, like grass.

The Operation

Sparse-haired, crumbling
teeth, your old mom
droops from the heat,
the pull on her teats
of a hundred infants.
A worn-out cat,
humped half to death,
she breathes decay
                    so Ruth
              we did it—
you wandered the house,
licked your neat nylon
stitches, your belly
shaved to velvet—

an early spinster
              a young old maid

as I recalled
an operation
in a glass-walled
room at a fair:
a doped dog, carried
in on a tray,
her womb removed,
the strange V shape
held up for the crowd,
knotted with pods
that were puppies . . .

and dreamed of
tiny paws & nails
pink underbellies
scraped-out bodies

the scooping of
ovaries   of
still-closed eyes
yet why
          if that's right
do you now
                    tomgirl
in boots
          chase
the Toms   rush
the tiger lilies
rub against us
singing   singing

as though you're not
dreaming of fuckings,
the taste of placenta,
as though you're not
laughing at my wires
to diaphragm, diapers—
as though you're not
questioning twenty
years of my life?

A Week in February

1

My host lies naked
in a field by a fence:
to make wine for my
breakfast   his wife
beats him with a kind
of swatter till his
blood runs. Hundreds of
children race about
the pasture   crying
"don't die   don't die."

she is frightened—
her ambition: is
it man-killing?

2

I'm cutting my naked lover's hair
in the bathroom. Suddenly
the scissors flash out to his prick.

she loves her love
she hates him—
she loves & hates
her need of him.

3

Inflated dolls: lifesize,
naked   with random tufts
of scraggly hair: someone
is showing me in an old
house empty of furniture.

daughters: will they go
naked because of
her alliance with
the devil, with power?

4

A wedding: two fat men
enter the church—
hold guns on us:
"Someone has raped
my virgin daughter—
drop your clothes—
we'll find out who."

I know who's guilty—
my dark father, son.
One slashes the legs
of a dark man, dissolves
his prick with acid.
I look over—my lover!
safe: light eyes, hair.

*the man who loves her—
unless protected
by magic colors—
will he perish?*

5

I have a son, a gorilla.
As large as I, he wrestles
me constantly. My lover says
I can give him away. *Release
release:* I haven't known it!

*because of her love's aura
—half-man half-woman—
her daughters are freed
she is loosed from night.*

Echoes from the Solitary Cell

1

I am holed up in this lookout
waiting for words. I whistle
in the crow's nest like an Eighth Dwarf.
Mockingbirds peck at my song,
mistaking me for some ordinary egg thief.
The days ignite each other
like a fence of dull matchsticks
that leads to a windy ravine.
In the windy ravine I just may find
a burning angel too transfixed
to explain what I mean.

2

We sing in our deep still wells.
If you dip your ear into mine
grace notes will nudge it out
like a litter of soft tombs.

3

In the solitary cell silence
rearranges itself into a fugue
that roots like steptococci
in the deaf ear. In the cell
an ear is an eye, an eye
is a tongue, a tongue is a heart,
a heart is silence, and silence,
the flesh I sink into my teeth.

4

The moon clicks like a broken
telephone. A stale cloud shrouds
Venus. You go here, you go there—
endless wires connecting the nerves of
America. Thank God we got TV,
she says to the walls of the solitary cell,
which hear
and wait.

5

Nothing is still in the solitary cell.
There is the pantomime of your shadow
unstitching itself on the walls.
The moon seeps in like gasoline fumes.
You set it on fire but
moons do not burn.
The door is open. You could
lead a life of pleasure
like a stolen machine
fibrillating in a cave.

6

Names and dates have been gouged
into the walls. They are all yours.
Your fingers are styluses of bone.
You place a pot of yellow flowers
on the window sill; you dust the bars;
you dig a hole and lie in it.
A gong drones in your chest.
If you sing the words you know
you will die. Your lips part slowly.
Words fall like BB's from your mouth.

7

The solitary cell is empty.
Moonlight rubs against three
stubby bars in the high window.
There are no skeletons or
devices of torture, no signatures
carved in the stone, no wedding rings
buried in the floor, no confessions.
Only the smell of ozone sweeping in
from ancient electrical storms,
the buzz of a spent transformer,
and a message. The solitary cell
signals like the finger of a patient
who cannot move or speak—but knows.
The solitary cell is never empty.

The First

Below a half moon
headlights twist
sultry pine dark.
Town after town
railroad-waste in the heart   the same
mansions blur to shacks to cotton
down the straight street   the same
canals   swamps   rivers   trees
Spanish moss   the same
stores   tobacco barns   the same

sudden shock
at the end of a continent.

Footprints out of season
unwashed by waves
root dunes.
Moonlight rides waves.
Moonlight falls with white tide walls.
Moonlight flies on the backs of gulls—
gliding gleaming troughs.

The first man to rise from sea
I try new lungs
speechless   gasping
spreading sand   trying again

and again to fill
long shadows.

Liquid moon
pours from the high horizon down.

Search for Victims

Accustomed to violent storms   they found
no precedents dictating that the creak
of wind in the eaves and the pop of raindrops bound
for roots were more than that   until creeks
brawled from their gutters like drunks. Mountains lost
their faces. Boards   tin   bones   all dispossessed shreds
of human existence smashed across
to the gorged river which rocked from its bed
through roads and bridges   wielding uprooted trees
like battering rams.
                        There will be time to live
when scars heal—time for townsmen to increase
their knowledge if their flesh is sensitive.
They search below flood-exhumed tissues tossed
to trees from which they droop like Spanish moss.

Stern Shapes

Stern shapes flying
through my childhood night
are harmless bats.
They come unscheduled
as I walk unsteadily
along back moments.
Though I duck
when first I hear their echoes
they remind me who I am
and call.
Paternally they swarm in
on their hard wide wings
that break my light
returning me to caves.
With blind fur pressed against me
I remember how to shriek
in their tongue
and rise with their dead certainty
in their dead night.

Burning

As it pumped the day like a bellows into its swollen lungs
the fire fanned up and down.
Until a finger poked through the hot wooden dyke to open air
no one saw sweat at the edge of fire
or sensed the boards nervous from rasping tongues
caught by an affection like unwanted love
which clings and sucks.

Flames worried the barn in spontaneous silence
until it blew up—
spewed timbers like lava from walls—
swept sheep down the barnyard
beneath black poisonous sky spraying sparks like confetti
down over the bucket brigade
who sang and sweated to death
giving water to fire.

Born in silence
hot larvae leapt down from the pipe in the hired hand's jaws
tunneled like rats through the hay and straw
breeding and feeding themselves on themselves and their litters
breeding themselves to cats to pursue
chasing up and over and under the beams
stretching liquid in mongrelized colors to rafters
to birds breeding and kicking themselves out of nests
to fly through breaks in the hot sided barn
to roost on cool rafters of neighboring sheds
or perch under floors   cackling   driving up
leaping to pig sties and barracks and corn cribs and wagon sheds
riding the horse herds to pastures and forest
whipping split fence rails and haystacks
vaulting back decades of trees to the lawn
as burnings fell into themselves
drawing tides like moons
draining water from ice ponds wells and pipes to the house.
Streams burned to their sources.

Fire came to my sleep
in sounds from behind a green shutter.
A feverish man
with burning eyes
touched me for water
feet rising and falling in flames
with a whine like the wind
in a wild forest head.

Fire came to my sleep
to wean me from land I never could own.
Like a mother it force fed me breast milk that boiled
for my temper.

I live by my temper.

I am tempered to dance
on an image which worries my feet.

Today

At last the time
of too much water
too little light
has passed.
The sky has burned off.
This is my birthday—
one I have never seen before—
one no calendar tells.
The pines are full
of unlit candles
about to flame
green into summer.
Glistening grackles
ride the swaying boughs.

Memorizing a Drowning

Hands meshed,
the chainlinked people
stretch out like a rope
into water, legs
trolling the bottom.
I watch, the lifeline
of my palms pulsing.
My toes erode the sand
& cling like barnacles
to safety.
Strapped in the undertow
the body sinks,
snags in thick sea weed,
breath snared in bubbles
that gurgle to the surface.

Swells of fatigue
sting my eyes like saltwater
as I drive back thru towns
on a mental highway of waves,
my hands clammy
on the night steering wheel.
In the headlights,
the body floats in,
white & bloated
like the belly
of an undernourished
child.

Fish Cleaning

When inlets are dragged
and fish netted,
tanned boys stride
on the dock like auctioneers,
barking their fees
in Italian accents.

As scales are scraped,
and fins and heads
neatly severed, a dream
swirls on the water's surface
in discarded eyes.

> Mermaids rake scaly hips
> against smooth thighs
> and swim away,
> sunning on rocks
> like vulgar photographs.

The shirtless boys
carry pails of skinned dreams
to the fishermen.
Paid, they laze in noon light,
scales glinting seductively
in their hairless navels.

All night the trains have passed

All night the trains have passed
keening their way through the
sleep-driven town.
When I close my eyes I can still see
the sun singeing the roof of the
post office, its windows crammed
full with red geraniums
letters grown stale with gray dust.
The house is not filled with us;
there is an empty space where our
bodies do not touch
though the sheets wrinkle limp
with our thrashing
and your fingers hang warm
at my throat.

Rowing

We all crept from the sea;
only the old oarsman is
not ashamed.

In the light left by morning
he separates the last day's
waves, savoring the salt
on his lips and coarse clothes
and pauses to salute with
raised net the young girl
standing dockside and dreamy,
fraying the mist with
her fingers.

Song for Susannah: A Lullaby

All the sun's peacocks are dreaming.
They have gathered their colors
and gone screaming to sleep,
swept up green shining gold
and a thousand indigo hearts
like cards when the game is done.

See how the day has grown weary.
It is an ancient gray man
taken to wandering
who shuffles his feet
and wears a ragged red sun
on a stick.

Do you not think that tomorrow will come?
Oh look, silly girl, how the birds have grown still
and the moon has wept frost on the leaves.

The moon, a clipped thumbnail

The moon, a clipped thumbnail,
is scraping the sky.
All day I have measured
the errors of time—counted
geese flocked skyward
children in gloves
skeletal trees mocking
shadows of leaves.

Night is uneasy.
I have come shyly for love
and hide hunger to hold you,
the curves of our spines
notching patterns in palms.

from Treasury Holiday
xxi

> If you don't like my peaches
> why do you shake my tree?
> If you don't like my peaches
> why do you shake my tree?
> Get out of my orchard
> & let my fruit trees be.

Ah

shit.

     Hips, hip-sockets, hip strength, inward & outward
     round, man-balls, man-root
not
in the 1st ed. (1855)

            Whitman had a dirty mind
In high school we read Leaves of Grass & Venus & Adonis &
     Look Homeward Angel & The Catcher in the Rye for their
     dirty parts
cummings had a dirty mind   Wolfe had a dirty mind   Shakespeare
     had a dirty mind   Chaucer had a very dirty mind
I have a very dirty mind indeed for I have breathed the same air as
     coroners
I have seen coroners' assistants with their stomachs & photographs
ball-headed men in glasses & plastics & synthetics & technical terms
(Ah   shit   in italics)
with stomachs of steel & bone buttons & stills of corpses

I saw one once of a young guy killed in a car crash
He was laid out on his back
Penis & testicles covered up by a little white rectangle

Laurence Sterne & Jonathan Swift & Samuel Richardson had dirty
    minds
Charles Darwin had a dirty mind & thought about shit all the
    God-damn time

& Benjamin Franklin & J. S. Bach & W. B. Yeats & Franklin
    Delano Roosevelt had dirty minds & were foul of mouth
Woodrow Wilson had one of the dirtiest minds in the world

Bloody Lydia Pinkham had a dirtier mind than the worst Lutheran
    convict lying on his left side in his grey cell thinking compulsively
    obsessively about pussy twenty-four hours a day day in day out
    seven days a week fifty-two weeks a year for his entire lifetime
    plus ninety-nine fiscal years for aggravated sodomy & high
    carnal knowledge
& if it's not pussy you can bet it's something even worse

But in the final analysis I think I would have to say that undertakers
    coroners & policemen have the dirtiest minds
& use the foulest language habitually
In high school they told us that the habit-forming use of profane
    obscene vulgar blasphemous language not only stank in the
    nose-drills of Yahweh but also indicated a deficient command
    of the English language
I guess that's right but still have never found a truer clearer or more
    forceful thing to call a son of a bitch than son of a bitch

Sean O'Casey (19 June 1950 Daily Worker): To hell with the atom
    bomb!
But old Allen Ginsberg with his dirty queer dope-fiend commie
    unbusinesslike mind says through his filthy antisocial
    objectionable obnoxious Jewish beard to clean upstanding &
    erect America: Go fuck yourself with your atom bomb.
Now how could that be said better?

"How could that be said better?" a nice old Ulster lady once asked
    me (the text in question being "gem of purest ray serene")
& so I honor her   I really & sincerely do

I honor her here by applying her praise to Ginsberg's scatological
    imperative
Go fuck yourself with your atom bomb

She was born in 1888 named Jane unmarried & my landlady in
    Londonderry
had been a schoolteacher & I don't doubt that she had given a
    great deal of serious thought to the mechanics & logistics of the
    operation of that place in the Miller's Tale where one guy
    gets back at another guy by shoving a red-hot plow-share
    up his ass
O plow & stars
& that reminds me that once when I was out she went into my room
    & took my copy of O'Casey's six-volume autobiography &
    later told me that O'Casey was dead that day in Turkey
I could not believe that but she explained (calling me Gorman
    because Harmon is somehow impossible in Gaelic she said)
    that Turkey was a place in Devonshire: Torquay

Ah   man-balls & root
Imagine all the ladies of the temperance & suffragette persuasions
    sitting & sipping bloody Lydia's vegetable compound which was
    one half booze & other half dope
thinking about the body electric & incleft outswell
Zip Zap snap crackle inward & outward round

my ass

        xxii

Now black katzenjammers are shooting up Newark
    (the metal shadow of Krupp slides down the wall
    as the light slides up/
                a run-thru for the System
                of LeRoi Jones's Hell
    the Krupp diamond slept through Elizabeth's hysterectomy)

blacks shoot up Newark
burning & doing a little looting
while whites shoot up Newark
burning & doing a little looting

pale Hans versus dark Fritz
    Vot der???!!!
            Vass iss?!?!?!?!?!
                there was the youngster

in old home town Chicago murdered the eight nurses
another young fellow did the Sgt. York routine at the University of
    Texas
    Donnerwetter!!

jawohl jawohl jawohl (click ankles) jawohl mein Führer

This is Niederschlag

vice murders versa all around the planet
Jew murders Arab, Sam murders Janet
you're smart to stay in the ground, Ernest Hemingway—talk about
    your dangerous summers
This ought to qualify

        i

I am the Gross National Product
absorb & including all things all goods Fab with Borax
Kleenex Clorox Kotex Kodak & Ex-Lax
I contain the spectacular car-crash death of the movie star
    Jayne Mansfield
& the quiet death of John Masefield the word star equally
the Baby Ruth no less than the Crab Nebula
I do not distinguish or discriminate the murmuring
of pine & poison The gross the great the grand National
pure products the good doc said go crazy
Lord God of Hosts I am the Gross National Product of the

United States of America & here celebrate the New Fiscal Year
this fourth of July in the Lord's anno
one thousand plus one thousand minus one hundred plus fifty plus
　　ten plus five plus three ones
in Mod. Am. Eng. ALFA DELTA 11110110000
I am the grand central Brother Jonathan & Uncle Sam
red white & blue-black all
I am first second & third persons singular & plural nominative
　　genitive accusative & focative
absorbing & subsuming all including Mister Fats Domino
Alexander Hamilton the handsome treasurer & Gaylord Wilshire
　　& Sylvester Graham & Mary Baker Eddy
O national product composed of compositions of all sorts of sorts
melting pot mulligan mulligatawny & huge buildings
& I reject the government as such for the government as nonesuch
& I categorically deny education religion youth communication love
　　industry poetry & all arts & sciences & games & nature & culture
all subordinated quite to one gross & national product in terms of
the lordly Long Green
money the only mother
money the only poetry
they say LSD in England pounds shillings pence O pounds of
　　money
money the only gross national poem & noumenon
for it is a good thing to me including all things & by its intermedia-
　　tion making them all holy one & all
the cheap ugly vulgar things
& language
holy body of money the only poetry
O gross & National bills coins post stamps lard futures bonds
　　vouchers gilt-edge blue-chip shares checks & military payment
　　certificates & rapid-transit tokens

ii

Now he is the Declaration of Independence a poem beginning with
    the rhyme When in
Now he is the Constitution a poem beginning with the rhyme
    We the
Now the Gettysburg Address a poem beginning with the rhyme
    Four score

iii

Atheist in religion anarchist in politics analphabetist in literature &
    good in all things I am myself everywhere
geography includes me & holds me cabined in its bosom
& I transcend the gross chorography to go plumb across coughing
    oceans on great circles & rhumblines in acorns & up the sky
    in steel seeds
go crazy products incorporated now fourth of Julius year of Jesus
neither congruent to us absolutely but included entirely herein
I grant Frigg her day
& pledge allegiance to the telephone
In motherfucker we trust
Computer the Gem of the Xerox
I'm stuffed from sea to shining sea with an immaculate gamut of
    supermarkets & fanes of ALGOL laundromats & left- &
    right-wingers & bluegrass clowns in union suits & gypsy
    babbitts & popular music
advertising cones & locofoco engineers & Queequegs & bimetallist
    homosexuals & abstracted seraphim & every e pluribus &
    quaquaversal thing
America O holy poetry the only Mary the only money

Mount Mitchell in North Carolina
at Dusk in October

Far ahead, the road curves through the blue trees
like the silver trail a boat leaves
on water.
The wake is breaking into the mute files of these trees.
In the sparse rain,
the glistening macadam extends even the faintest light.

High on the mountain,
one tree stands taller than all the rest.
It leans toward the upward part of the mountain.
Its branches all point upwards.
They grow only on the high side of the tree.
The other side is bare,
its bark struck off by a lightning bolt.
Now it stands, looking brave and terrified.

The mountain is loud with the sounds of dew.
Every rock face weeps teary beads, rivulets
run into beds worn into rock and soil,
between roots, in ditches by the roadways.

I drive higher and feel colder air.
I round a hairpin curve. An elegant buck leaps
so close I hit my brakes hard. His handsome rectangular
hindquarter disappears in the thicket
and then the doe, her fawn behind her,
arches across the road in two bow-shaped leaps
into the woods.
All three disappear into silence.

At the top I stop, drive around the parking lot,
then leap onto a wall
and look into two hundred degrees of blue distance.
A car comes up behind me.
A boy in a wheelchair, a man and a woman get out.
No one speaks.

The mists keep rising from hidden but imagineable valleys.
The mists look like the tops of seas
which are turning gaseous
between the water they rise from
and the air.

On the Dock at Oak Bluffs

Once we saw the sun setting behind us,
We walked nearly backwards along the dock.
The sea to the east was turning evening gray-green.
The sky westward was like a frozen camera flash.

But then a crowd of fishing poles and people
Huddled around a drama their close company hid
Turned us away from the sun to the discovered shark,
His mouth opening then shutting, a sea-wolf
Brought to land, twisting like a fallen crescent moon.

A boy decided to flip him back into the sea.
No one knowing what to do, he broke a common dismay
By deciding. I remembered a dock by a cold stone
Bluff on Maine's coast twenty-five years before, a sand
Shark like this one landed, then clubbed to death.
Then, that was all that anyone could think to do.

Extensions of Watts Bar Dam

Here where bass flip and stagger
to a dazzle of slow blue water
carp dive to alluvium where human

divers won't swim. Locals will say
catfish bigger than men sleep there,
just waiting. But the current is plenty

to keep men in boats; logs, buried
in bottom silt, bloom free, swivel,
then splinter against the wall.

The dam itself is a postcard on which
an official writes by the lights of dials
an afternoon's program for the river.

Through the turbines, the idiom
picks up, becomes the thrumming song,
the giant's voice in chains,

the housewife hears— about how
the water spills everything: obscenities,
threnodies, or no, how the current

catches fires, races through vacuum
cleaners, sewing machines, mixers.
Or it is all in dreaming. The faces

of shoals are locked under a lid
of water and the key has been lost.
Now Oak Ridge burns in the cobalt

distances, and we know no anodyne
to ease that pain
or the beauty of this river

curving in its sheath
like a long blue scimitar
running too deep to return.

Debris

At last, the pillows would take our heads
Which have held all day the thoughts of nothing
In particular, only we have wanted
So much of girls and grace, an understanding
With the wind, a kinship with white houses.

And all evening, it has seemed there have been
Too many words, but none specific enough.
The convoy passed, containing young reserves,
The jokes they told escaped us
While rain unsnapped samaras from the elm.

It was a day of wobbly passes thrown at our feet,
Of softballs yellowing just beyond
Our outstretched gloves, and we would release
Those hours at once, like tickets or tamed birds,
We would lie down without voices, without nerves.

But for some time, our oaths have softened
Against the plaster; the lights thinning out
For miles, and echoes returning, old, diminished,
Their aspirates scuffed on sand rock
Or hung in the moist branches of the hydrangea.

Until it seems all this year has been
A dim window and snoring from another room.
Debris of my days, untouchables, I think the moon
Sent down your code, but I could not read it.
I give this calling to get you back again.

The Fern

Grandmother, fat witch of my childhood,
Today I potted the fern that flourished
For forty years in your strange sun.
A plant in a roasting pan, a plume of green
Brought from the mountain when you married:
The only tender sign I ever knew you guilty of
While, longing for cities and for sons,
You rode my grandfather's nights
Into days of daughters. Cheated of dreams
You imperiled us all with your madness—
My crazy aunts, crazy mother, crazy self—
Gnawing the hot radish of hate, while we,
like fattened hens, clustered and clucked,
"Love us." Like the hens whose necks
You whirred above your head, we flapped mindless—
Anguished because your tough hand
Ignored the dark life that flowed out
On country dirt.

What lives we had we spun outside.
What love we found, we somehow hid,
And when you died I said "Give me the fern."
We divided goods, sold the land, moved to town.

All the tokens, willed and scattered, are gone.
The house, oaks, vineyards;
The barn and its cat; gone
The skittering shade of your anger.
There is left this green monument
Which, like me, is a faint reminder
Of powers dominant in their hour
Worlds ago. But this fern, monstering
Only my living room, remembers nothing of that,
And nothing at all of you.

The Pireaus Apollo

In 1959 workmen of Pireaus, port city of Athens,
cut too deeply into a sewer and found a number
of precious statues, among them Apollo 6th C. B.C.

Were they singing, the workers,
the anonymous dark angels,
as they raised you
from the long waters
beneath the sewers of the port?
Did they sing, did they sing
as they brought you forth
to bring us the sea's messages,
the tide's agreements, the pacts
made with the patient ages?
Did they know what work
they worked from the sewer's
secrets, from the dark
of the cold sea?
Did they sing, did they sing
as they raised you
shining to the sun
as they brought you
to show what the clear gaze
looking inward knows,
what the calm mouth cherishes?

The Woman in the Next Room

With each pain
She screams at God. Though the door
Is shut and nurses try to quiet her
With talk, I hear her howling
For salvation. Another pain
Begins: I grip the bed, feeling
The flesh grow tight, intensely
Mount until I cannot breathe
To cry aloud; an alien head
Locks firm in the bones
And I and the woman in the next
Room are sisters in madness.
The white sweep of the clock
Shortens our breathing; a face
Sealed in a green mask peers
Down at me, looms in my nightmare
Like a rational voice. Doctors,
Midwives of living practice their deep
and hidden art while the women
They fear suffer and hasten
Their death. Oh sister, madness
Becomes us: these Gods are mortal,
We must endure them. Pain
And forgetting: the clock
Brings us closer to that hour
When we cheat death
With our bodies.

A Formality of Love

So locked in ice
your body burns.
The frozen flesh
of your mouth,
splinters of teeth,
even the buried steel
of your tongue
coming up through
the ice
wary
as a fish.

She Calls from Shore

Once more you call, but the black and vicious tide
turns out to sea, the barnacles exposed.
I am out beyond the last exacting breakers,
past swimmers with their grease still heavy
on the foam. My bones weave in the arctic night,
down the narrow straits where the dolphins
dream under ice.

Shall I swim back, command the sea to empty?
My scales will turn to flesh, my eyes to fable.
Queen, Mother, I have no home but this sick water.
and what reflections of the land I see
are but a glint of those dumb fish
singing on your hook.

Spring

The can turns black around the apple juice.
Dogs fucking in high grass
are visible as ears, unusually juxtaposed.
Later one will run, and one lie down, and nothing show.

A pregnant woman holds
her breasts as she mounts
stairs, descends stairs.
In the long garden near her room dirt folds

rain through to the seeds. Nobody counts,
nobody counts. It is unbearable to think it.
I am a pregnant woman. You lie in high grass somewhere.
The juice will darken in its well until I drink it.

Leaving

Between your lips trees grew like words.
Your tongue got too flowery. You went on
and on like Virginia until I was unheard
of, a name plowed in your mouth for fertility to set upon.

I hope I never see anything grow
undisciplined, unshaped again,
cypress dressed up in moss, in mud below.
I am not of your kind, the gentle men

who hold the wooden handles and the bare
blades of verbs but do not mean them.
I am the new woodsman, who will spare
lives, thin them, lean them,

whack past gardenfuls of harvesters and hurt,
have an axe in my mouth, the word desert.

Sayings

Islands don't sink. They are not spirits
and they are not ships. They do not
try to float: it is this accomplishment
of indifference which comforts
the lonely man in a Tidewater town, unlike
what misery loves, that family
of resemblances, brood
of sympathies. I'd rather
have you, says the lonely man,
who have given up your likenesses, your mooring.

Here the flat-bottomed boats rub up
on shoals and women shapes,
phrases and friction
of tongues, growl
of gravel and spit. In the distance,

small and fat and striped—boy,
low, lub, bob, bell—
the independent
syllables are floating.
But with effort. Meaning
deeper risk.

The Elephant

Ziggy, a 55-year-old elephant, starts to ascend a gravel ramp from the 10-foot moat which surrounds his cage at the Brookfield Zoo near Chicago. Ziggy fell into the moat Sunday and spent more than 24 hours there before being freed. He broke a tusk and cut his head in the fall. It took two tow trucks and a 24-member rescue team eight hours just to turn him over on his stomach. When keepers called to Ziggy and offered his favorite food, he ignored them. A keeper had to jiggle a door leading to Widget, a female elephant, before he would move.[—Story with A.P. Wirephoto]

Whether his advancing middle age
spoke to him of tigers
or of the boy who fed him soap,
now himself grown bald,
or whether a small hand held too far
away the proffered peanut
and he, to please a child,
strained a step beyond good sense,
the elephant has fallen in the moat.

His gray bulk is wedged against wet, gray walls
like so much old cheese.

He, Ziggy, Killer Giant, Star of Stars;
He, on whose back Ziegfeld's beauties danced;
He, pride of the Brookfield Zoo;

He, an old, fat, senile pachyderm
is on his back, stuck fast,
his tusks splintered.

But an elephant never forgets
and the girls still dance in his glazed eyes
to remind him
that he will not budge for tow trucks, hay,
or twenty-four man rescue squads.

Only the clank of a young cow's chain
will inspire him
again to walk the jungle of his dotage.

Frog's Lament

My tongue aches from a summer of extension,
flexing;

wet heat and fetid muck,
mosquitoes, leeches day and night,
the soft feet of the fox,
the raccoon's paws:
my quickness my strength,
I have survived them all.

Now nights spill into mornings,
the pumpkin sun slants chill.
My legs unbend with effort, now;
I do not walk much.

Around still writhe
my own spilt milt,
my legless progeny,
spermatazoa grown Gargantuan
in a snake dream:
lungless, gaping heads and tails,
the gift of my lust to the world.
They remind me

it is October. Veins constrict,
oaks drop flame
onto the pond's still surface

and I, cold, unfulfilled
turn to the mud's warm womb.
We will be colder soon, and stiffer.

The Vinegar Jug

It's on account of you,
I start the day off drinking,
sucking my bitter sop,
preening pretty fur.

I might tame a wild animal
to appreciate me,
to lick my paw, gaze at me with sweet dull eyes.
But I might never clear the land—as you have done—
of beasts and creeping things,
make it safe,
squeeze its wine
in the right wine-season.

These are the shining chains
you make for me.
A man and his wife living in a vinegar jug,
and they were happy.
He sang to her some songs,
each note dying and reforming
in its brother.

At night she rubbed her feet,
smiling at the gold shackle
around the petty bone.

Lumbee Children

They are like figurines.

I am in the presence of relics,
treasures from the Inca pyramids.
So I tote the sight of them
like bright jewels
in my uneasy mind.

Their names come across the desk,
dull, tame as any enlisted English muster.
I hope for one Standing Bear among them,
one Cochise,
one dazzling Coyote-Man.
They don't give me any.

Not a feather, a bead,
not a string,
not one ragged buckskin.
They came out of the pyramids
no older than the day
they went in.

I want to arm them,
give them the bow, the fancy repeating rifle,
the beautiful bomb.
They should have it.

But these are figurines,
turning in the sun,
feeding that ancient uneasy star.
Somewhere,
the priest in the pyramid
has already raised his knife.

To My Neighbor
and Almost Namesake
Shot by Strangers
While Walking His Dog
and Among His Flowers

The loss I admit is soon lost.
Each day a *Constitution* or a *Journal*
Lies on the lawns that grow for the mowing.
Now dogwood distracts from the burnt azaleas.

None of your money was taken with your life.
Bleeding away through twenty hours,
You were able to identify your assailants,
Though none was known to you before that morning.

Perhaps the color of their eyes was singular;
Triggered your mind the instant that they shot you,
As you reached back behind you for your wallet,
Knowing you had to pay for unexpected visits

But not how much. We had missed meeting
Exactly by a letter and one street.
Friends who mistook z for a t rang up,
Were reassured and left congratulations.

Grieved, I was not, nor much ashamed by luck;
Moved for a moment that moved on—new flowers,
My house in a dead-end street,
And no dog to walk in the early hours.

Path Under the Medlars

Autumn how far exceeds our expectations
overfilling the barns and still
the brown mash of windfalls
under our feet and the air
overburdened with apples

The wild fruit of abandoned trees
bringing the boughs down before
white cottage doorways. Everything breaking
and the wasps too glutted to fly

but in frenzied circles knowing no way out
of impossible surfeit. October, November
and, long after apples, the medlars
overripe in the skins and everywhere
musk of medlars. And why is this year so
generous? Why only to trees no one has tended

these hundred years? Walking dark ways
in the rain and the raindrops sweetened and
colored like sap and the smell lingering, tell me
were we too prudent? Were we? Let everything go.
Let the years go. Let love that most
overhusbanded, overwifed thing Go!

At Withers' Swash

*"On his tour south, President George Washington spent the night of April 27, 1791 near here at the home of Jeremiah Vereen, revolutionary patriot, where he was 'entertained (& very kindly) without being able to make compensation.' The next morning Mr. Vereen piloted the President, en route to Georgetown, across Withers' swash on the strand now called Myrtle Beach."**

You can see the two of them on horseback,
riding leisurely to the swash:
G. Washington and J. Vereen.

Eighteenth century sunlight on the leaves
flickered in the calm hope of discipline
and the tall spear-shaped grass bent back

and sprang beneath their horses' bellies.
The wind blew up the smell of myrtle,
and the strong salt odor of the flats,

earthy and serene, was in their grasp
as what was most essential in themselves
and in each other. Washington

went on to Georgetown on the sandy road
winding past Long Bay, through the yuccas
and the flies stinging, and that eighteenth

century freedom rippled on ahead of him
like the sunlight scintillating on the
stiff but pliant stalks of marsh grass,

or the smell of beach wort in the wind
that tastes of lemon when you bite it,
and he waved farewell to J. Vereen.

* Highway sign on Route 17, South Carolina. Withers' Swash is now the site of the South's largest roller coaster.

Washington, Diseased

If I could only settle my intestines,
put my kidneys and my gall to order
I could show those British Army snots

what it means to be a Virginia gentleman.
The bloody flux I got fighting their wars
was enough shit, without theirs

even if I killed the French ambassadors,
setting Europe on its end for seven years.
When you come right down to it, that's no more

than I've sat bloodying for my sins
another pot. At Fort Necessity I learned
the man who wins must have patience

with causes. And what the cause is
of this disease, which also makes me cough
and wheeze, I know not, although my brother

Lawrence died of phthisis.
Once, in the mountains, I watched the mist
blowing up a cliff and forming droplets

on the mullein and on my hat.
Now while the French and British fight it out
I'll look for better devils in myself.

Perhaps they'll destroy each other
and I'll be well again on my own account.
If not, the Virginia earth will heal me

and I will rest the better for their help.
Sometimes it seems a century since this fight
I started in the wilderness first began

and mist and Indians both skulked
up from the rivers. I've seen
the Appalachian range a hundred miles

of smoking valleys, and the dark hills
rising from the mist like whales
until they faded into greyness. The rod

I've kissed was made of oak. But if I live
I'll take a mattock to the root, whether French
or British, in this century, please God.

*Note: In 1754 Washington fired on a group of French carry-
ing ambassadorial credentials, triggering the Seven Years
War. The French retaliated by attacking Washington at
Fort Necessity; and he was forced to withdraw. In Novem-
ber, 1757 he came down with the bloody flux, which brought
him close to death. He was then twenty-six. He did not re-
cover until March, 1758. One of the great disappointments
of his life was the refusal of the British to offer him a com-
mission in their regular army.*

from Paula

4.
Paula steps softly
on the circles of the light.
The circles made by drops on the bougainvillea.
Drops of water or drops of light
confusing wetness and dryness
as the petals
    confuse leaves with petals.
The circles
are circles of confusion
like the sparkles of insects
confusing the water with their size.
She steps carefully on the drops of light
circling her feet
    as though as definite as insects
both in quantity and weight.
She steps carefully among the circles
as in the spines

of cactus that fringe her yard.
She leans against the terrace carefully
looking into the distance of the cactus-
studded cliff
which drops in circles of light.
She can see
   the road winding to San Sebastian.
The white road that makes circles
in the rain that never falls,
around each drop. Above all
there are the circles of the bougainvillea
which are like poppies
in their lightness.
They catch the wind
   which is making circles on the ocean.
They catch dew, to make
circles of the water.
They catch the light
in order to make people
appear and disappear within the silence.
The circles of the light are over
everything. They hold the whole island
in a certain
         relationship.
Judging its shape,
   choosing sites for villages
and letting roads
wind slowly through the valleys.
There are some villages above the roads
that do not need a road.
And people call by whistling
in circles of sound
   from one mountain to another.
Paula listens carefully
to the circles of the air
becoming the circles of light
around the bougainvillea.

She is a goddess among the goats.
She is a goddess among
   the radishes.

The Old Men

(Thoughts of a Young Girl)

Why do they never speak, the old men,
Leaning behind banisters when I pass?
Staring from rotten porches, they rock,
Dry sticks between thin legs,
Drooling snuff. I see their naked tongues,
Lizard eyes that gulp me in the heat.

Or at stores, hunkered on blue salt licks,
Their brittle fingers shake, fumbling at flies.
They grin. Why will they never speak?

I never look back, once gone—
But feeling their eyes on me like a stain,
My flesh shrinks close to the bone.

Afterwards

on the way back
from the deep woods
(the boy gone)

three martin gourds
writhed on the cross
under low skies

and dry sunflowers
(all of them)
turned dark heads
to the path
accusing her

The White Stallion

(The Runaway)

A white horse came to our farm once
Leaping like dawn the backyard fence.
In dreams I heard his shadow fall
Across my bed. A miracle,
I woke beneath his mane's surprise;
I saw my face within his eyes,
The dew ran down his nose and fell
Upon the bleeding window quince. . . .

But long before I broke the spell
My father's curses sped him on,
Four flashing hooves that bruised the lawn.
And as I stumbled into dawn
I saw him scorn a final hedge,
I heard his pride upon the bridge,
Then through the wakened yard I went
To read the rage the stallion spent.

The Blessing

He is surrounded.
He knows he must yield.
His sons line up like hollyhocks
along this bed's bright field.
Their sturdy flesh blooms white
inside his eye. At his feet
a cluster of daughters spreads like
a ripe still-life. Their cheeks,
their breasts, the shadows cupped
into each nape of neck: they are fruit
he has grown, his tongue can almost
taste them.

One by one now we make a last procession.
To each, a Lear aged past all possession,
secure in this kingdom of pain,
he whispers: You. You were my favorite.
You were. Always.
It is something he repeats.
He savors the taste of our names,
though he will not recall this secret confession
when the next child enters.

I've heard his refrain, seen it laid
in my brothers' and sisters' palms
like a silver dollar. I bend to kiss
the tender spot beneath his starched
pajama collar. And know I'm too late.
You, he says. You.
He must convince me now,
but it is finished.

Father, Father, I want to say,
I will never complain.
That word alone is a blessing.
Your blood sings in my veins.

Delta Summer

My grandmother likes to tell about
when she was young and thin and
the levee broke
and the flood came over
the leaning town
like a dirty wave,
toteing horses and shoes and rings
and a few Negro men
who happened to be there
fishing their supper
when the waters sighed
and rose up.
She likes to tell about
how she tucked up her long white
skirts and climbed barefoot to the roof
alone, to watch, like a bird, the river
suck through trees and how
she heard the cattle and chickens
choke.

My grandmother lies in her bed
like a bloated queen,
painting her pointed nails,
her hair the color of rust,
and tells me this,
her watery eyes
as soft as fish:
how the mud was black
on the gate posts for weeks,
and how ten children
drowned that day
in the middle of
the oak-lined residential street.
Their graves, she says, are
quaint black stones
that lie beneath the concrete wall
which keeps the waters neat
today.

To the Children Selling Lightning Bugs

They rush
against a glass dome,
wounding each other.
Light dribbles off them
like blood.
Wings are eyelashes,
batting against light,
their own light,
bleeding.
Like bombers
kamikazeing into darkness
darker than they know,
they fall.
Their batteries slowly weaken.
Blink.
        Blink.
A signal to the fleet,
those sparks that hover safe
as neat harbor signs,
under the willow, upside-
down beneath moonflower vines.
Blink.
We are breathing a curtain of air,
we are finished with flowers,
finished with leaves. Blink.
Our engines are leaking,
our muscles are torn
from the sleeves of our wings.
Come to us quickly.
Come.
We are burning alive
in this pouring light,
in our own sweet blood.

Burning the Letters

After twenty-three years
of being unable to sound
the strokes of her name,
twenty-three years
that have scattered her dust—
kneebones, wristbones, all—
over wild lake water,
today you are burning
her letters.
You climb to the attic night
where the crisp words
glow in the dark.
Below in the slow green light,
I am your waiting target.
Though the sunlight smokes around us,
inside the boxes you bring
Chicago's winter air has blown
into flowers. Beneath, her letters
wait, little pigeons whose folded wings
will break into powder finer than snow
under our fingers' tracks.

This much you say you can finally do,
since now I'm the string that ties
your minutes each to each
and will not unravel.
I'm the stray who follows you everywhere,
I take morning from your hand.
But under my fingers her round hand
moves, searches for you still.
She writes, "When will you come?"
Not knowing you can never,
even now, find reason to leave,
or to burn away the traces
of her touch.

The Majorette on the Self-Rising Flour Sign

We came each day to where
You had been laid
In tall grass behind the football field,
Twice again as large as any half-time majorette.
Where you once stood and smiled beside our practice field
Some more comely figure had reared herself
To suggest we try her snowy white self-rising flour.
But she stood beyond our ready grasp;
You waited in easy weeds,
Offering the self-same flour.
Although your soldier-girl suit was out of style
We rose to the red, white, and blue of your flower,
Imagined ourselves clasped
Between your flaking white thighs,
And peeled the red away to see
What secrets lay beneath your uniform—
We found the galvanized lie,
Slowly peeled you all away,
And went to other flower fields.

From where we sit tonight
We do not see your skeleton in the weeds.
New floodlights now blaze above us
And players from another generation
Prepare their kick-off on this worried ground.
Dutifully we rise for The Star-Spangled Banner
And over the loudspeaker a prayer comes
For good clean sports.
Behind the top-row bleachers on less familiar signs
Are this age's superwomen,
Their painted smiles saying merely someone has the ball.

And now as half-time majorettes cover the grid
We go to the sideline cables for a closer look.
A new routine is announced.
But when the floodlights go off
Nothing new comes; our bloodshot eyes

Reject the dark, begin to probe beyond the field,
Catch on something, snatch and seize a form that parts
    the grass—
In our flaming hands on these retaining wires
We feel an old charge now current our night,
For you arise from those self-same weeds
And under goal posts take flesh
And come to where we hang on cables,
Breathless.

You pitch and toss across the field
And at the end throw your fire batons
Into the night—
We watch with galvanized eyes
As you come again full-fleshed
In these half-times of our lives.

Water I Thought Sweet and Deep

The quail are flying wild
And those we've killed begin to smell
So we turn toward home
On a day too hot to hunt.

At some stranger's dog-trot shack
We ask if there is water we might drink.
A raw-eyed drunken man offers from a Mason jar
The same white whiskey that rings his rotten jaw.

We decline and find his well—
I draw and drink until
I see swimming in the dipper
Flukes in water I thought sweet and deep

Flukes swimming grey against the tin
Before I throw them straight into the sun
Take his jar   drink what smells of kerosene and month-
    old egg
Breathe deep and sweet in my hunting bag

And retch until each organ wrings
Itself of water
Quail death
Whiskey I thought sweet and deep.

No Man's Good Bull

No man's good bull grazes wet clover
And leaves the pasture as he came.
My uncle's prize Angus was bloated
And breathing hard by afternoon
On the day he got into our clover pasture
Before the sun could burn the dew away.
He bellowed death from the field
As we grappled to hold his legs and head;
Our vet inserted a trocar between his ribs,
                let the whelming gas escape,
And to show us the nature of that gas
Put a match to the valve . . . a blue flame caught
        and the animal bolted from us,
Heading into the woods along the river bottom,
Turning only to test the new fire
                of his black side.

Each night we see his flame, blue and soft
                        beside the river,
As he steals in before dawn
To plunge his head into wet clover,
Graze his fill,
        blaze up,
And answer that which lows to him in heat.
We watch him burn—
            hoof, hide, and bone.

Grabbling in Yokna Bottom

The hungry come in a dry time
To muddy the water of this swamp river
And take in nets what fish or eel
Break surface to suck at this world's air.

But colder blood backs into the water's wood—
Gills the silt rather than rise to light—
And who would eat a cleaner meat
Must grabble in the hollows of underwater stumps and roots,

Must cram his arm and hand beneath the scum
And go by touch where eye cannot reach,
Must seize and bring to light
What scale or slime is touched—

Must in that instant—on touch—
Without question or reckoning
Grab up what wraps itself cold-blooded
Around flesh or flails the water to froth,

Or else feel the fish slip by,
Or learn that the loggerhead's jaw is thunder-deaf,
Or that the cottonmouth's fangs burn like heated needles
Even under water.

The well-fed do not wade this low river.

Waking Under Sun

This morning of my Easter exile
the lake catches fire with the sun.
Rippled reflection snares a solo crow blazing.
"Craw, craw, craw," the fire bird cries.
Blue Ridge peaks hang duned with snow
in my memory like lodestones calling.

I step from the net of my nylon hammock
to the shore where silver water
tastes the twisted weeds and slaps.
A lost tourist prying day open
like a stubborn history nut, I yawn for coffee.
Morning flexes itself, a golden muscle,
through my unfocused image stretching.

All lakes lead to the sun,
the yellow spar of light that scorches.
I learn from the light in its context.
Barbs of waves in the water
furl and fist in the wind,
looping mountains on the lake:
Swanless, wakeless, green as lynx eyes.

My eyes uncrust to the spangle and roll
of wet fire, a sea of blazing sparks
leaping. Ever the sun,
God's own god,
braids coiled around his crown.

My waking goes unnoticed by crows
or the oaks they sway with their perching,
and the flat stretch of yellow sky
unwinds its binding threads.
Staring at the solar star's gold skin,
I remember the crisp rattle
of a mountain stream on brittle sticks,

a masked coon scratching bark,
and the baying of beagles in the moon.

My knife's silver edge splays venison,
sawing strips from the hart to hang like tongues
over a blistering fire of withered sticks,
and the Ra-faced sun cooks shadows
on the lake as cool as foil.

Afternoon brings its rain like silver blood
clicking on summer leaves.
A thin lake falls from the cloud-masked sun,
and lightning jags mountains in the sky,
to the west, in the dusk, on the breeze.
In the east, a lone star rises.
Somewhere wise men see stars in the mountains
where deer like shadows sip from a still stream
and amulets of mica preserve this light.

Double-Header

Each and every one of us has a schedule to keep.
—a truck driver being interviewed on radio

I've made it
have been left alone in the stadium
locked here after the baseball
twilight game, having hidden
where I won't tell

on a bet with someone I invented
and therefore had to win.
I can hear the Security Guard
locking up, watch him making his way out,
turning off the lights as he goes

toward home and supper, away from
the smell of popcorn and beer.
I can see him look
with a question at my car,
the only one besides his

still in the lot and see him
look back once at the stadium without
knowing or even thinking I could be
looking back at him, my face barbed
with wire. I turn now to the stadium

that is all mine, bought
with my money, purchased with
a three dollar ticket for the top tier,
the stadium that is coming alive again
with the crowd that is coming back

but of course isn't coming back
to watch me play, with DiMaggio in center,

Cobb in left, Hornsby at second,
Rizzuto at short, and all the others
who have been tagged out more than once

themselves, and who will get me later

or sooner, trying to stretch a single
into a double, catching up with my lost breath
that I can remember now from when
I was eleven, with a stitch in my side

sprinting still in spite of the stitch
for the inside-the-park home run
I almost had when I was twelve
for the girl I almost got when I got
old enough but didn't know the rules

dusting my pants off now
to the music I never learned, for
the symphony orchestra I never conducted,
my hands rough with rosin
for the truck I never drove

and the fish I never caught
and wouldn't have known if I had
how to take him off the hook,
for my father who is in the crowd
cheering out his heart

but who of course isn't there
as I pull up lame at second
with a stand-up double
in this game that goes on for hours,
my hands stinging with the bat,

the All-Stars aligned against me
in this stadium I own for the night,
one great circle and inside this circle
this square that seems the only one
on this curving darkening ball of earth

or the only one anyway
marked by bases I must run all night
for everything I should
by now
be worth.

Looking Down Into a Ditch

Watching the workmen dig a ditch
watching them lay in the pipe

for the waste and gasses
and liquids of our living

I think of the lost maps
of lost cities, their pipes
still moving off
in important directions

of people I knew
who are now in the serious dirt

of the ditches at Dachau

of my father.

It is hard
to keep remembering
across the ditches we have made
and covered over
with terrible earth-moving sound

how much of our dying
we must find ways not to need,
how much of what keeps us alive
is underground.

Losing a Voice in Summer

How many parts rumble it was
how much gravel
dark, light
I don't remember

and it won't echo for me
from the shower stall

though sometimes off the porch
calling my own sons for supper
I can almost

almost hear it

as if you had let it go
out of the corner
of your mouth
like a ventriloquist
without a dummy.

I have no recording

otherwise I would play you
in the shower, repeat you
off the porch

from the cat-walk
of the glass factory have you sing
Go Down Moses
over and over and

tonight
with the reluctant sentence
deep in my head at the hoarsest hour,
dumb and laryngitic and alone

I first understood
how completely I have lost your voice,
father, along with my own.

Marthy

I know why they kept you poor and cast
you with the children and the dafter servants:
you were beautiful a fact recorded
in the dusty fall of 1897.
Caroline and Nannie
each married the same man
passed the pride of bearing sons
from one to the other. Omitting you.
A changling. No pie-faced Scottish lass surely.
Surely the sheened and tapered daughter
of a rich Polish Jew.
Through a Great War and a Great Depression
your mournful letters beckoned the brother/cousins
home to Christmas and Easter.
Finally there was only you.
In your dresses long as trousers
eyes like blackened silver.
You wound your lustrous hair to strings
planted on the light of the moon
what should have gone to ground on the dark.
The brother/cousins slipped the shrinking matrix.
The suburbs cropped the land.
They say I stir a pot like you
my knees and ankles inept in company
my arms too flimsy fingers to flexuous
for the pitcher. But I am not beautiful
not alien enough in my looks
to have dusted the decent mantles til they cracked
do not have the fearful purpose
to wear deserted porches like a shawl
grace a staircase's uncoiling.
What you must have seen in your flights
past the dusty mirrors of that barren place.
Undone. Gone to ground both.
The house pulled down made parking
for the reservoir.
The boys they recalled

your maelstrom eyes your taut mouth over the boiling pot
grin and glitter under the man's hat
leaning lamplight the hiss
you could have been their mother.
They laid you with Caroline and Nannie
in the square with the tallest obelisk.

Quest

She, posed periwinkle
To the waist, before
A gaunt Rooms-with-Board house
Or, silk-fringed shawl wrapped,
Leaning against a woods
The color of dried blood
Or, figurehead for ships
Bound for ports he'd not
Dreamed. She ended his bold
Search, never begun.

He, content to be a
Shadow, lay beneath
Her shoes to catch her face
Backangled on her
Stem of a neck. He came
From the loveless clutch
Of maiden aunts through France
Axle deep in war
To "Twenty-three skiddoo!"
In a bleak milltown.

And in the picture book
Reposes the freshness
He thought he'd found, not sought.
Like a recurring dream
Turned meaningless, and dry
As the sepia
Of a country road.

Arrival

What do you love
A voice said
Myself

Where does that get you

These are the wrong questions

My daughter has begun
To linger with pages
To sleep under her pillow
Collect flies   She has told
Me
The snow is black under the mountains

She lives elsewhere
My son
Addresses the light as though he would dance
With it
He requests messages
His eyes
Read me in no language I understand
They are his
Partner

Often when the evening
Forgets its hour and the day turns
Into itself my wife
Remembers
The years before me
She keeps her
Distances

I would have it no other way

These are the wrong answers

They are not answers

Where does that get you

Here

Major Work

When I died
The light around me   that
Mold
Cracked
Fell away

Such dust arose
As would accompany
The breaking of vows

It ascended so finely
Shattered
It seems whole

A sky
Under which I began

Again

The Trial

I thought it was over

The reporters began
Leaking out of the courtroom
Bars crept up the windows
The tanks in the street shriveled

I began to breathe
The echo of doors
Locking   my judgment

It was a relief

I anticipated the mornings
Their cold dust
The stone growing in my head
All my life I thought
*Will be the same day wound
Into itself   the same night*

I thought it was over

But when I turned
Robes glittered above me
I rose into them
Taking my soft place
Among the judges

New Year's

I have walked this whole road
How many times
Past imagining
And never surrendered

No one was ever armed
But I have my own thorns

It is not as though there were beasts
Either
But I keep my threats ready
Like a net

I asked the mirrors
For directions

They all point the same way

When was it I turned to you
And heard the ditches sing
Farther?

I took it for a promise

But you see
How accurately the footprints wait
How carefully they weather

Remaining

Saving the Barn

I dream of stones
and stumbling through them
a lost child   lovers   a stray

finding a field
and at the far end
that wild fading clump of a barn

the kind you cut a finger to own
and sign in blood.

There is more shuttered in and out of sequence
    the fragrance of damp bodies bumping into sleep
    from the loft a shout
    murmurs feathering down
    and myself
    lying here   weathered.
Minutes   hours   years later
the barn burns
and I wake
on fire to rush in and save what I can

the children who are still hidden
abandoned and closed

the children who have grown to be mine
and the lover I slept through   burning
while my ashes lifted with the wind and died.

This is what it means to rain
and hard ground not hold.
This is how it is to be a tree
pressed into stone.

A man I could love wanders by and touches me.
I throw myself in his eyes

and make tears come.
He leans on my body
but the ashes are spread too thin
and he passes through.
I settle
on flowers that are carried home.

Rabid

Night comes
and what is the point of closing our eyes?

Howls leap at the fence
one howl lunging at another
connecting streets   towns

howls
gnawing at sleep
while you shift against me
conditioned not to wake

your arms across my breast
your tooth on my jugular.

Howls.

The door to the room is locked
but what of the nightmare
twitching between us

a loop of saliva
swinging from its lip?

Frayed Sheets

We stand across from each other
About to fold
The bedsheet between us.
We notice the edges, frayed.
I want to apologize, I don't know why,
For the years we lay together
Offering our sleep to the night,
Sacrifice to the god of dream.

Yesterday, in the attic,
You found your wedding gown.
It too was frayed, though it hasn't
Been worn for years.
Soon, its lace will turn to snow,
Something to brush away with our hands
When we tire
And lie upon the earth.

Look into my eyes,
If you can see that far
Across the white expanse between us
Where my voice has left
The silent tracks of its echo.
Forget the sheet, it is not skin.
Wearing it through
Exposes nothing of each other's life.

Frayed, or tattered,
We can simply fold this sheet,
The flag of our private country:
A bed we can lay down our lives upon,
And never rise, strangers.

Surgeon's Prayer

His hands are stronger
Than her whole body

As they sew up the cheek
Of a nine-year old girl.
His lips move
In a silent recital of calm

Against the stitch (resembling
One crescent of
A parenthesis, as if a thought
Were to never end,

As if his words were only
To be heard as gradually
As the skin healing.

Crazy Horse

In the moon of exploding junipers
Tashanka Witko
Crazy Horse
warchief of the Oglala Sioux
went alone
into the Black Hills
and had a vision
what he saw
after a week of fasting cold
projected in the sundance of the stars
were numbers
numbers of the dead
lines of escape
angles of attack
geometries platonic
pure as moon abstractions
on new snow so
accurate they were
prefiguring
nobody laid a glove on him
counted coup
on him once
removed from mortality
he was not himself
not Tashanka
who hunted for a living
gambled on moccasins
teased children
but one who had dreamed
himself out of himself
and had felt his horse float
under him
like a butterfly.

The Hunt

The field are caricatures of themselves.
There is always the effeminate riding instructor,
aftershaven, his bat in his boot,
a horse depending from his saddle,
a Tom Buchanan, a Vronsky, and all
the virgins who popped it over fences. Come
this nebulous November morning
to fly a double oxer and bore through bullfinch
the rest are as good as unhorsed already.

But at a distance, a black-and-tan,
draped in the rags of their breath,
astride geldings of no color,
they are as indistinctive as
the pack of wall-eyed foxhounds
that casts about this fallow pasture
in concentric circles
of metronomic lope.

There is only the fox:
cadaverous   unpredictable   wedge
of sinew red as dried blood, hounded
by the thick musk of his mortality
that cannot be blown away or frozen.

The Autochthon

if it was Clinch Valley, Virginia
you'd figure:
James Stephens
was a Meulungeon,

some kin to the famous Morning Glory Finch,
half-Indian/half-Raleigh's-Eden,
gone back to
ground . . .

but this is Newton County,
Arkansas Ozarks—
place with overhill towns
name of Parthenon, Ben Hur, Red Star,
Yellville, Verona, Snowball . . .

James Stephens lives in the woods:
one billy goat, two dogs, assorted ents,
one black cat

he plays the concertina for them
late at night
in women's clothes . . .

"You Are My Sunshine"—
contra natura

he often misses his dinner
that they may eat

"You Are My Sunshine"—
contra natura

on the table,
along with these photographs by Cherel Winett,
is an epigram
by Edward Dahlberg:

"I abhor the cult of the same that is the universal malady today,
and acknowledge I'm different, since I came into the world
like the four elements:
emotion, strife, remorse and chagrin."

I'd like to see James Stephens take a picture of Richard Nixon,
or Richard Avedon, from back in there where those eyes of his are—
a place, with topsoil in the character

the face
looks like J. Paul Getty
without a dime,
with character

the last face I saw anywhere near its equal,
that was Clarence Schmidt's, he
was sitting in the derelict car in the Wonder-Garden
on the Ohayo Ridge near Woodstock:

"call me Clarence, boys!
you from some sort of foundation?
—no, no use writing a poem, NBC's already did it,
screened it all over California . . .
bad thing too—these hippies come,
steal me blind . . .
yes, well, help yourselves, I got to fix thishere foil icicle
tree, see . . ."

like Old Man Turley Pickleseimer,
who hid out from the Guvmint during some war
in a cave down in Blue Valley,
which became known as 'Pickleseimer Rock House,'
I hope James Stephens stays hid,
plays his goat-songs,
stays off tv and out of Fort Smith

as you know, Stephen Sykes,
of Aberdeen, Mississippi,
made the mistake of going into Memphis one night and later remarked:

"Don't talk so much.
Keep your mouth
closed
and your bowels
open,

and believe in
Jesus!"

Dealer's Choice and the Dealer Shuffles

(for William Burroughs)

I saw the Chattahoochee River get a haircut.
I saw Fidel Castro flow softly towards Apalachicola, Florida.

I saw a bank of red clay integrate with Jesuits.
I saw Bob Jones Bible University used to make baked flamingos.

I saw the Governor of Mississippi join the NAACP.
I saw a black gum tree refuse to leaf and go to jail.

I saw the DAR singing "*We Shall Overcome!*"
I saw Werner von Braun knitting gray (and brown) socks
    for the National Guard.

I saw the Motto of Alabama: "IT'S TOO WET TO PLOUGH!"
I saw God tell Adam: "WE DARE DEFEND OUR RIGHTS!"

I saw the City of Albany fried in deep fat.
I saw eight catfish star on Gomorrah TV.

I saw "THE INVASION OF THE BODY-SNATCHERS" at the
    Tyger Drive-In
I saw William Blake grow like a virus in the sun.

I saw the South suckin hind titty.
I saw the North suckin hind titty.

I saw a man who saw these too
And said though strange they were all true.

Postface:

'*There was a crow sat on a clod—*
And now I've finished my sermon, thank God.'

Dear Reverend Carl C. McIntire:

Just a note
to let you know
we are listening to you
on Station
K-I-K-E
in Richmond,
Virginia

There are four of us Fundamentalist Baptist ladies
who ride to work together at 7:30
to the shirt factory and the napalm plant
and we always listen to your
"20TH CENTURY REFORMATION HOUR"
every day
after the early morning
"MO-TOWN-SOUND-SHOW" with
"Urethra & the Catheters"—

you both groove, baby,
I mean you let it *all* hang out
and no doubt!

So when you laid that wicked-world bit
on our heads Friday we felt we should be prepared
to meet God and goodness we sure would feel lost
without your spiritual uplift in our new pink
Dodge Polara . . .

Yours agin sin and keep keeping those darkies
from destroying our freedom,
zang-a-dang!

Myrtle Jean Pugh, Co-Captain
James River Industrial League of
White Women Bowlers,
Team #16

Who Is Little Enis?

Little Enis is
"one hunnert an' 80 lbs of
dynamite
with a 9-inch
fuse"

his real name is
Carlos Toadvine
which his wife Irma Jean
pronounces Carlus

Carlos says
Toadaveenie is a eyetalyun name,
used to be lots of 'em
around these parts

Ed McClanahan is the World's Leading Little Enis Freak
and all this information comes from a weekend in Winston
with Big Ed telling the lore of Lexington, Kentucky,
which is where Enis has been hanging it out for years and years,
at Boot's Bar and Giuseppe's Villa and now The Embers,
pickin' and singin' rockabilly style

Carlus ain't what he was
according to Irma Jean's accounts
(and even to his own):

he was sittin' there one night in the kitchen at home
tellin' stories and talkin' trash about Irma Jean—
with her right there with her hair put up in them pink plastic curlers—
about how these days how he likes to pop it to her dog-style
just now and again and how she likes it pretty damn well
when they wander all over the house
and end up in the living room corner—
"I'm just afraid Carlus will run us out the door and down the street
opposite the automatic laundry . . ."

The 9-inch fuse hung down Enis's left leg
is called, familiarly,
Ol' Blue

Ol' Blue used to be in the pink—
way in

Blue had a head on him like a tom-cat
and ribs like a hongry hound

and he used to get so hard
a cat
couldn't
scratch it . . .

but now that Enis has the cirrhosis
and takes all these harmones
Ol' Blue just don't
stand up like a little man
and cut the mustard
anymore

but Enis will smile and say
let's all have a drink, maybe I can drown thatthere liver of ours,
it's no bigger'n a dime nohow anymore, it just floats in there . . .

Hey, Blue, let's shake that thing!
Turn loose this oldie by my boy Elvis,
a golden oldie—
let's go, Blue!

And off they go
into the wild blue
yonder in the Blue-
Grass . . .

Carlos & Blue
thinking of you . . .

hail & farewell!

January

In some other life
I'll stand where I'm standing now, and will look down, and will see
My own face, and not know what I'm looking at.

These are the nights
When the oyster begins her pearl, when the spider slips
Through his wired rooms, and the barns cough, and the grass quails.

Equation

I open the phone book, and look for my adolescence.
How easy the past is—
Alphabetized, its picture taken,
It leans in the doorway, it fits in the back pocket.

The crime is invisible,
But it's there. Why else would I feel so guilty?
Why else would that one sorrow still walk through my sleep,
Looking away, dressed in its best suit?

I touch my palm. I touch it again and again.
I leave no fingerprint. I find no white scar.
It must have been something else,
Something enormous, something too big to see.

At Zero

In the cold kitchen of heaven,
Daylight spoons out its cream-of-wheat.

Beside the sidewalk, the shrubs
Hunch down, deep in their bibs.

The wind harps its same song
Through the steel tines of the trees.

The river lies still, the jewelled drill in its teeth.

I am glint on its fingernails.
I am ground grains on its wheel.

Indian Summer

The plains drift on through the deep daylight.

I watch the snow bees sent mad by the sun.

The limbs of the hickory trees swing loose in the noontide,
Feathery, stretching their necks.

The wind blows through its own hair forever.

If something is due me still
—Fire dogs, ashes, the soap of another life—
I give it back. And this hive

Of sheveled combs, my wax in its little box.

Next

I am weary of daily things,
How the limbs of the sycamore
Dip to the snow surge and disaffect;
How the ice moans and the salt swells.
Where is that country I signed for, the one with the lamp,
The one with the penny in each shoe?

I want to lie down, I am so tired, and let
The crab grass seep through my heart,
Side by side with the inch worm and the fallen psalm,
Close to the river bank,
In autumn, the red leaves in the sky
Like lost flags, sidle and drift . . .

Morandi

I'm talking about stillness, the hush
Of a porcelain center bowl, a tear vase, a jug.

I'm talking about space, which is one-sided,
Unanswered, and left to dry.

I'm talking about paint, about shape, about the void
These objects sentry for, and rise from.

I'm talking about sin, red drop, white drop,
Its warp and curve, which is blue.

I'm talking about bottles, and ruin,
And what we flash at the darkness, and what for . . .

Sentences

The ash fish has been away for a long time now,
The snow transparent; a white cane rakes back and forth
In the hush, no sweet sound from the leaves.

———

Whatever is dead stays dead: the lighted and cold
Blue blank pavilions of the sky,
The sand, the crystal's ring in the bushy ear—
Voices logy with sleep, their knapsacks
The color of nothing, full of the great spaces they still must cross.

———

The trees take care of their own salvation, and rocks
Swell with their business; and there, on the clean cloth
Of the river, a Host is floating without end.

———

Heaven, that stray dog, eats on the run and keeps moving.

THE AUTHORS

JAMES APPLEWHITE was born August 8, 1935, in Wilson County, North Carolina. Educated at Duke University, he is currently Associate Professor of English at Duke. He has received a Guggenheim Fellowship in poetry for 1977. His volume of poetry is entitled *Statues of the Grass*.

COLEMAN BARKS was born April 23, 1937, in Chattanooga, Tennessee. He was educated at the University of North Carolina at Chapel Hill and the University of California at Berkeley. He is an Associate Professor of English at the University of Georgia. He has published extensively in literary magazines. His collection is *The Juice*.

DAVID BOTTOMS was born September 11, 1949, in Canton, Georgia. He was educated at Mercer University and West Georgia College. His poems have appeared in magazines such as *Prairie Schooner, Kansas Quarterly, Southern Poetry Review,* and *Midwest Quarterly*. He has an active interest in bluegrass banjo and guitar, and is an editor of Sweetwater Press.

JOHN CARR was born in Mississippi in 1942. He was educated at the University of Mississippi, Hollins College, and the University of North Carolina at Chapel Hill. He has published poetry, fiction, and nonfiction in *Georgia Review, Virginia Quarterly Review, Southern Poetry Review,* and *Intro. 6*. His book of interviews is *Kite-Flying and Other Irrational Acts*.

FRED CHAPPELL was born in Canton, North Carolina, in 1936. He was educated at Duke University. He is a Professor of English at the University of North Carolina at Greensboro. He has received grants from the Rockefeller Foundation and The National Institute of Arts and Letters. His books of poetry and fiction are *It Is*

Time, Lord, The Inkling, Dagon, The World Between The Eyes, The Gaudy Place, and River.

KELLY CHERRY was born in Baton Rouge, Louisiana. After growing up in Ithaca and Richmond, she studied at the University of Virginia and the University of North Carolina at Greensboro. She has been an editor, a private tutor, and a writer in residence at Southwest Minnesota State University. Her books include a novel, *Sick and Full of Burning*, and poetry, *Lovers and Agnostics* and *Relativity*.

ROSEMARY DANIELL was born November 29, 1935, in Atlanta, Georgia. In addition to her involvement with the Callanwolde Poetry Committee, she has conducted poetry workshops and has worked extensively with poetry in the schools projects. Her collections are *A Sexual Tour of the Deep South* and *The Feathered Trees*.

LOUIS GALLO was born in New Orleans, Louisiana, in 1945. He was educated at Tulane, The University of New Orleans, and the University of Missouri. He teaches at the University of New Orleans and edits *The Barataria Review*. His poems and stories have appeared in *Kansas Quarterly, Mississippi Review, North Dakota Quarterly*, and *Tales*.

ROBERT WATERS GREY was born October 12, 1943, in Sandy Spring, Maryland. He was educated at Brown University and the University of Virginia. He is an Assistant Professor of English at the University of North Carolina at Charlotte. His poems have appeared in *Kansas Quarterly, Southern Poetry Review, Western Review, North Country Anvil*, and *Eleven Charlotte Poets*.

TIMOTHY HAMM was born September 29, 1954, in Concord, North Carolina. He is a student at the University of North Carolina at Charlotte and a weaver in Cannon Mills. His poems have appeared in *DeKalb Literary Arts Journal, Star-Web Paper*, and *Miscellany*.

DORIS HARDIE was born July 7, 1954, in Burlington, North Carolina. She was educated at the University of North Carolina at Charlotte. These are the first publications of a promising poet.

WILLIAM HARMON was born in Concord, North Carolina, in 1938. He was educated at the University of Chicago, the University of North Carolina at Chapel Hill, and the University of Cincinnatti. He is a Lt. Commander in the Naval Reserve and the chairman of the English Department at the University of North Carolina at Chapel Hill. His books are *Treasury Holiday, Legion: Civic Choruses,* and *Intussusception of Miss Mary America.*

THOMAS HEFFERNAN was born August 19, 1939, in Hyannis, Massachusetts. He was educated at Boston College and the University of Manchester. He is poet in residence for the North Carolina poetry in the schools program. In addition to editing various anthologies, he is the author of *Mobiles and Other Poems.*

RODNEY JONES was born February 11, 1950, in Hartselle, Alabama. He was educated at the University of Alabama and the University of North Carolina at Greensboro. Having worked with poetry in the schools programs in Tennessee, Virginia, and North Carolina, he now lives in Bean Station, Tennessee. His poems have appeared in *Southern Poetry Review, Kansas Quarterly, The Greensboro Review,* and *Shenandoah.*

BARBARA LOVELL was born October 11, 1932, in Charlotte, North Carolina. She was educated at the University of North Carolina at Greensboro and Vanderbilt University. Her poems have appeared in *Contempora, Southern Poetry Review, The Cold Mountain Review,* and *Women.*

ADRIANNE MARCUS was born March 7, 1935, in Everett, Massachusetts. After growing up in Fayetteville, North Carolina, she was educated at the University of North Carolina at Greensboro, Campbell College, Shorter College, and San Francisco State

University. She teaches at the College of Marin. She is the author of *The Moon is a Marrying Eye* and *The Photojournalist: Mark and Leibovitz.*

HEATHER McHUGH was born August 20, 1948, in California and grew up in Gloucester Point, Virginia. She was educated at Radcliffe College and Denver University. She is an Assistant Professor at SUNY, Binghamton. Her work has appeared in *The New Yorker, Harper's, Atlantic,* and *Antioch Review.*

DOUG McREYNOLDS was born June 5, 1946, in Shreveport, Louisiana. He was educated at the University of Missouri. He is a fellow at the University of Denver. His poems have appeared in *Miscellany, Tar River Poets, Veins,* and *Colorado Quarterly.*

HEATHER ROSS MILLER was born in Albemarle, North Carolina, in 1939. She was educated at the University of North Carolina at Greensboro. Currently, she teaches at Stanly Technical Institute. Her novels, short stories, and poems are *Tenants of the House, Edge of the Woods, Confessions of a Champeen Fire Baton Twirler, A Spiritual Divorce,* and *Horse Horse Tyger Tyger.*

MICHAEL MOTT was born December 8, 1930, in London. He was educated at the University of London at Royal College, Oxford. Formerly active in London publishing, and a former poetry editor of *Kenyon Review,* he is currently Writer in Residence at Emory. His collection is *Absence of Unicorns, Presence of Lions.*

P. B. NEWMAN was born May 12, 1919, in Chicago, Illinois. He was educated at Antioch College, the University of Iowa, and the University of Chicago. He is a Professor of English at Queens College, Charlotte. In addition to his work in multi-media, he has published four books of poetry, including *Dust of the Sun* and *Paula.*

GUY OWEN was educated at the University of North Carolina at Chapel Hill, Utah State College, and the University of Chicago. He is a Professor of English at North Carolina State University and is the editor of *Southern Poetry Review*. His works of poetry and fiction include *Season of Fear, The Ballad of the Flim-Flam Man, A Journey for Joedel, Cape Fear Country,* and *The White Stallion and Other Poems*.

JESSIE SCHELL was born in Greenville, Mississippi, in 1941. She was educated at the University of North Carolina at Greensboro. Her works include one novel, *Sudina,* as well as short stories and poems in *The Greensboro Reader, The New Orleans Review, Atlantic,* and *Vanderbilt Poetry Review*.

JAMES SEAY was born January 1, 1939, in Panola County, Mississippi. He was educated at the University of Mississippi and the University of Virginia. He teaches at the University of North Carolina at Chapel Hill. In 1968, he was awarded the Emily Clark Balch Prize for poetry. His books are *Let Not Your Hart* and *Water Tables*.

R. T. SMITH was born April 13, 1948, in Washington, D.C. and grew up in Griffin, Georgia. He was educated at the University of North Carolina and Appalachian State University. He teaches at Auburn University and is the founder/editor of *The Cold Mountain Review*. His book is *Waking Under Snow*.

JOHN STONE was born in Jackson, Mississippi, in 1936. He was educated at Millsaps College and the Washington University School of Medicine. His first book of poems is *The Smell of Matches*. He sees patients and teaches at Grady Memorial Hospital and the Emory School of Medicine in Atlanta.

NANCY STONE was born December 23, 1934, in Erwin, North Carolina. She was educated at East Carolina University, the University of North Carolina at Charlotte, and the University of North Carolina at Greensboro. She is an Assistant Professor of English at UNCC. Her poetry and fiction have appeared in *Sunstone, Worksheet, The Greensboro Review,* and *The Iowa Review*.

DABNEY STUART was born November 4, 1937, in Richmond, Virginia. He was educated at Davidson College and Harvard University. He has taught at William and Mary and is currently a Professor of English at Washington and Lee University. His books are *The Diving Bell, A Particular Place, The Other Hand,* and *Friends of Yours, Friends of Mine.* He is the poetry editor of *Shenandoah.*

JULIE SUK was born in Mobile, Alabama. She teaches at the Charlotte Nature Museum. She collects shells and mines gems. Her poems have appeared in numerous literary magazines. Her first volume of poetry is *We Lie Here Itching.*

ROSS TALARICO was born March 17, 1945, in Rochester, New York. He was educated at Wisconsin University and Syracuse University. He is an Assistant Professor of English at Loyola University in Chicago. His books of poetry are *Snowfire* and *Simple Truths.*

MARVIN WEAVER was born September 12, 1944, in Decatur, Alabama, and grew up in Tuscaloosa. He was educated at the University of Alabama. Having taught writing and television production workshops for the Soul City Foundation, he is currently Executive Director of the Arts Council of Fayetteville. His first book of poetry is *Hearts and Gizzards.*

JONATHAN WILLIAMS was born March 8, 1929, in Asheville, North Carolina. He was educated at various places, such as Princeton, Phillips Memorial Gallery, and Black Mountain College. He is an essayist, the editor, publisher, and designer of The Jargon Society. His books include *An Ear in Bartram's Tree, Blues & Roots/Rue & Bluets, The Loco Logodaedalist in Situ,* and *Mahler.*

CHARLES WRIGHT was born August 25, 1935, in Pickwick Dam, Tennessee. He was educated at Davidson College and the University of Iowa. He is a Professor of English at the University of California, Irvine. His books of poetry are *The Grave of the Right Hand, Hard Freight,* and *Bloodlines.*

White Trash has been cast in hot metal on the Linotype and printed letterpress by Heritage Printers, Inc., Charlotte, N. C. The text type is W. A. Dwiggins' Electra in roman, italic and cursive. The paper bears the watermark of the S. D. Warren Company and is designed for an effective life of three hundred years.

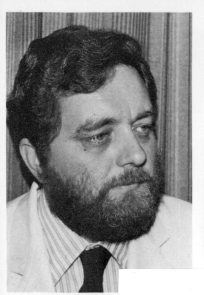

Kelly Cherry

rvin Weaver

Do

Nancy Stone

Dabney Stuart

Heather Ross